Software Craftsmanship

Software Craftsmanship

The New Imperative

Pete McBreen

ADDISON–WESLEY

Boston • San Francisco • New York • Toronto • Montreal
London • Munich • Paris • Madrid
Capetown • Sydney • Tokyo • Singapore • Mexico City

The publisher offers discounts on this book when ordered in quantity for special sales. For more information, please contact

Pearson Education Corporate Sales Division
One Lake Street
Upper Saddle River, NJ 07458
(800) 382-3419
corpsales@pearsontechgroup.com

Visit AW on the Web: www.awl.com/cseng/

Library of Congress Cataloging-in-Publication Data

McBreen, Pete.
 Software craftsmanship : the new imperative / Pete McBreen.
     p. cm.
 Includes index.
   ISBN 0-201-73386-2
 1. Computer software—Development. I. Title.
   QA76.76.D47 M386 2001
   005.3—dc21

                                    2001040041

0-201-73386-2
Text printed on recycled paper
1 2 3 4 5 6 7 8 9 10—MA—0504030201
First printing, August 2001

To the Management
Lesley
and her assistants
Bethan and Jake

Contents

Foreword

This book asks some tough questions.

Is software engineering appropriate for projects of less than 100 developer-years? Is the specialization inherent in software engineering a good idea? Can software development even be expressed in engineering terms?

It also asks some sensitive ones: Are less experienced developers paid too much, and should senior developers be paid more than almost anyone else in their organization? Should tools that are less than ten years old be used on long-term projects?

And at its heart, this book asks the big question: How can we reorganize the process of building software so that it works?

The book has some controversial answers: It suggests that we've lost sight of a simple truth—large methodologies and formal structures don't write software; people do. To fix a growing crisis in software development, we need to start by producing better developers. To do that, Pete looks back to a system that has worked well for hundreds of years—craftsmanship.

Craftsmanship is far more than a tag for high-quality work. In the full meaning of the word, craftsmanship is a self-sustaining system in which masters arrange for the training of their replacements and where status is based purely on the work you've done. Apprentices, journeymen, and craftsman all work together as a team, learning from each other. Customers select these teams based on the team's reputation, and teams accept only work that they feel will enhance their reputation.

Can this full system of craftsmanship work in our industry? Frankly, I don't know. Many entrenched interests will certainly oppose the idea. But I *do* know that being apprenticed to masters works. It worked for me.

I was lucky enough to attend a great university, where I learned much theory (there was less theory back then). What really made the experience shine, however, was an apprenticeship that I served. One of the graduate students took me under his wing. He didn't explicitly teach me, but he showed me by example how a great programmer thinks. Working next to him month after month, I absorbed more practical knowledge about design, coding, and debugging than any course could impart.

Later, I joined a start-up in London where I served a different sort of apprenticeship. My new boss showed me that software development was as about people as it was about technology. He helped me understand the business side of the equation and taught me how great development builds personal relationships from a base of technical strength.

I "graduated" from these two very different apprenticeships a far, far better developer than I started out. Based on my personal experience, I'm a believer. Working with masters is the best way to learn a craft.

This book offers more than ideas about training the next generation of developers. It is also about a philosophy. Craftsmanship stands for taking personal responsibility: for your work, for your personal development, and for your profession. It doesn't matter how you develop software. You could be working 9-to-5 in a CMM level 5 shop, or you could be pulling 100-hour, caffeine-drenched weeks developing the next cool first-person shooter. You could use RUP, XP, or SCRUM—or no process at all. Whatever the structure of your work, the real value in software development is added when skilled developers write high-quality, appropriate code, delivering what the customer needs. Methodologies don't produce these skilled developers. Honoring and practicing craftsmanship, along with the other ideas in this book, just might. You'll do yourself and your career a favor if you spend some time with Pete McBreen's tough questions.

David Thomas
The Pragmatic Programmers

Preface

Craftsmanship is a return to the roots of software development: Good software developers have always understood that programming is a craft skill. Regardless of the amount of arcane and detailed technical knowledge that a person has, in the end, application development comes down to feel and experience. Someone can know all of the esoteric technical details of the Java programming language, but that person will never be able to master application development unless he or she develops a feel for the aesthetics of software. Conversely, once a person gets the feel for software development, the specific technical details become almost irrelevant. Great developers are always picking up and using new technology and techniques; learning a new technology is just a normal part of the life of a software developer.

The term *software engineering* was coined in 1967 by a NATO study group that recommended a conference to discuss "the problems of software." The report from this 1968 conference, which was sponsored by the NATO Science Committee and took place in Garmish, Germany, was titled *Software Engineering.*[1] In the report, Peter Naur and Brian Randell stated "The phrase 'software engineering' was deliberately chosen to be provocative, in implying the need for software manufacture to be based on the types of theoretical foundations and practical disciplines that are traditional in the established branches of engineering."

In the same spirit, it is the intention of this book to be deliberately provocative in implying the need for practitioners to start paying

---

1. Naur, Peter, and Brian Randell, (eds.), *Software Engineering: A Report on a Conference Sponsored by the NATO Science Committee*, NATO, 1969.

attention to the craft of software development. Software craftsmanship is important because it takes us away from the manufacturing metaphor that software engineering invokes and makes us pay attention to the people who do software development. Craftsmanship brings with it the metaphor of skilled practitioners intent on mastering their craft, of pride in and responsibility for, the fruits of their labor.

Software craftsmanship is not the opposite of software engineering or computer science. Rather, craftsmanship is a different tradition that happily coexists with and benefits from science and engineering. Just as the modern blacksmith benefits from better tools, materials, and understanding, so software craftsmanship benefits from better computers, reusable components, and programming languages. Just as blacksmiths transcend science and engineering with their skill and artistry, software craftsmanship can transcend computer science and software engineering to produce great programs, applications, and systems. UNIX and the modern-day GNU Linux are probably the best-known examples of this—systems that are thriving due to the craft, skill, and dedication of their creators.

Software craftsmanship is a response to the problems of trying to force-fit software engineering into commercial application development. Software engineering was developed to meet the needs of NATO in developing very large defense systems. Commercial application development differs from the development of defense and government systems in that applications are a whole lot smaller and normally have to be up and running in less than 18 months. It is rare for a commercial application to be developed by a team of more than 20 people, and most application developers work in teams with fewer than 10 members. Software engineering is good at handling the problems of really large teams of 200 or more people, but it has little to say about how the individuals in a team should practice their craft.

Software engineering encourages the "human wave"[2] approach to software development. Rather than solving the problem of how to develop highly skilled developers, software engineering attempts to

---

2. Levy, Steven, *Hackers*, Penguin Books, 1994, p. 88.

deskill software development by suggesting that every problem can be solved by throwing more people at it.

Although this approach sometimes succeeds, the resulting software is junk. Slow and bloated, it just never feels right. Users are dazzled by the graphics and animation but never really manage to come to grips with the software. They are thwarted by their inability to learn the software and use only a small fraction of the available features.

Software does not have to be like that.

All too often I see application development teams shipping valuable applications that provide real, measurable business benefit, but apologizing for not following software engineering best practices. For me, the real test of a team is whether it manages to ship and then enhance and extend the application for years afterward. Timely shipping of the first release is important, but it is more important that subsequent releases occur in a timely fashion and that each new release improves the application.

Whenever I'm asked about hiring developers, I tell people to look for developers who have shipped a few applications successfully and then stuck around long enough to handle the next enhancement or maintenance release. Shipping proves that the developer can make something work; staying around for the next release allows the developer to experience the effects of the way that he or she built the application in the first place. If a developer has done this three times, my guess is that he or she is skilled and experienced enough in the craft of software development to be successful again.

Software craftsmanship is the new imperative because many members of the software development community are starting to chase technology for its own sake, forgetting what is important. The purpose of software development is to create high-quality, robust software applications that deliver value to their users. What matters is growing a new generation of developers who can do that.

Software craftsmanship stands for putting the joy and excitement back into creating applications for our users.

PART 1

Questioning Software Engineering

<hr />

Is the software engineering approach the best one to use when developing software?

Yes and no.

Some projects are well suited to the software engineering approach, but most are not. Software engineering was invented to tackle the problems of really large NATO systems projects. These projects pushed the state of the art in both computer hardware and software development for that new hardware in the late 1960s and early 1970s.

In 1968, a NATO conference identified a *software crisis* and suggested that for large, high-quality software applications, software engineering was the best way out of that crisis. Since that time, the needs of the U.S. Department of Defense have dominated the conversation about software engineering.

So, yes, you should look to software engineering if you have a really large project that is creating innovative computer hardware and you need software developed. The lessons learned by NATO should be applicable to your project.

Of course, the U.S. Department of Defense is not the only customer for software. Today, commercial applications, Open Source software, application packages, shrink-wrapped software, and interactive computer games are all pushing software development away from the classical software engineering approach. Their emergence suggests that it is time to reevaluate the way that we develop software.

Once we start reevaluating how we do software development, it becomes obvious that software development is not a mechanical activity; thinking of it as engineering is a mistake. Instead, we need a better metaphor: software craftsmanship.

Chapter 1

Understanding Software Engineering

In order to understand software engineering, we first need to look at the projects that were reported in the early software engineering literature. One feature is immediately striking—the absence of reports on commercial applications. Most case studies are of either large defense projects or small scientific projects. In either case, the projects typically involved severe hardware and software challenges that are not relevant to most modern projects.

A typical example is the SAFEGUARD Ballistic Missile Defense System, which was developed from 1969 through 1975.[3] "The development and deployment of the SAFEGUARD System entailed the development of one of the largest, most complex software systems ever undertaken." The project took 5,407 staff-years, starting with 188 staff years in 1969 and peaking at 1,261 staff-years in 1972. Overall productivity was 418 instructions per staff-year.

SAFEGUARD was a very large software engineering project that challenged the state of the art at the time. Computer hardware was specially developed for the project. Although the programming was done in low-level languages, the Code and Unit Test activities

---

3. Stephenson, W. E., "An analysis of the resources used in the SAFEGUARD system software development." In Donald J. Reefer, *Tutorial: Software Management*, IEEE Computer Society, 1981.

required less than 20% of the overall effort. System Engineering (requirements) and Design each consumed 20% of the effort, with the remainder (more than 40%) being accounted for by Integration Testing.

The Paradox of Software Engineering

In trying to understand software engineering, we need to keep two points in mind:

- Projects the size of SAFEGUARD are extremely rare.

- These very large projects (1,000-plus staff-years) helped to define software engineering.

Similarly, *The Mythical Man-Month*[4] by Fred Brooks was based on IBM's experiences when developing the OS/360 operating system. Even though Brooks wrote about the fact that *large programming projects suffer management problems that are different from the problems encountered by small ones due to the division of labor*, his book is nevertheless still used to support the ideas behind software engineering.

These really large projects are really *systems engineering* projects. They are combined hardware and software projects in which the hardware is being developed in conjunction with the software. A defining characteristic of this type of project is that *initially the software developers have to wait for the hardware, and then by the end of the project the hardware people are waiting for the software*. Software engineering grew up out of this paradox.

What Did Developers Do While Waiting for the Hardware?

Early in the typical software engineering project, there was plenty of time. The hardware was still being invented or designed, so the software people had plenty of time to investigate the requirements and produce detailed design specifications for the software. There

---

4. Brooks, Frederick P., *The Mythical Man-Month*, 20th Anniversary Edition, Addison-Wesley, 1995.

was no point in starting to write the code early, because the programmers lacked hardware on which to run the code (and in many early examples, the compilers and loaders for the code were not ready either). In some cases, the programming language wasn't even chosen until late in the project. So, even if some design specifications were complete, it was pointless to start coding early.

In that context, it made sense to define a rigorous requirements process with the goal of producing a detailed requirements specification that could be reviewed and signed off. Once the requirements were complete, this documentation could be handed off to a design team, which could then produce an exquisitely detailed design specification. Detailed design reviews were a natural part of this process, as there was plenty of time to get the design right while waiting for the development of the hardware to advance to the point where an engineering prototype could be made available to the software team.

How Did Developers Speed Up Software Delivery Once the Hardware Became Available?

The short answer is, "Throw lots of bodies at the problem." This was the "human wave" approach that Steven Levy described and that can be seen in the manpower figures reported from the SAFEGUARD project. As soon as the hardware became available, it made sense to start converting the detailed design specifications into code. For optimum efficiency, the code was reviewed to ensure that it conformed to the detailed design specification, because any deviation could lead to integration problems downstream.

Lots of people were needed at this stage because the project was waiting for the software to be written and tested. So, the faster the designs could be converted into tested code, the better. Early software engineering projects tended to use lots of programmers, but later on the emphasis shifted toward the automatic generation of code from the designs through the use of CASE tools. This shift occurred because project teams faced many problems in making the overall system work after it had been coded. If the code could be generated from the design specifications, then projects would be completed faster, and there would be fewer problems during integration.

Implications for the Development Process

Software engineering projects require lots of documentation. During the course of a project, three different skill sets are needed:

- Analysts to document the requirements
- Designers to create the design specifications
- Programmers to write the code

At every stage, the authors of each document must add extra detail because they do not know who will subsequently be reading the document. Without being able to assume a certain, common background knowledge, the only safe course is to add every bit of detail and cross-referencing that the author knows. The reviewers must then go through the document to confirm that it is complete and unambiguous.

Complete documentation brings with it another challenge: Namely, team members must ensure that the documents remain consistent in the face of changes in requirements and design changes made during implementation. Software engineering projects tackle this challenge by making sure that there is complete traceability from requirements through to implemented code. This ensures that whenever a change must be made, all of the affected documents and components can be identified and updated.

This document-driven approach affects the way that the people on the project work together. Designers are reluctant to question the analysts, and the programmers may be encouraged not to question the design nor to suggest "improvements" to the design. Changes are very expensive with all of the documents, so they must be controlled.

A great way to control changes from the bottom is to define a project hierarchy that puts the analysts at the top, with the designers below them, and the programmers at the bottom of the heap. This structure is maintained by promoting good programmers to become designers and allowing good designers to undertake the analysts' role.

The Modern Definition of Software Engineering

Over the last 30 years, the software engineering community has followed the path of applying mechanical metaphors to the software development process. Software engineering is now an accepted academic subject and an active research field for universities. The focus for software engineering projects is on a defined, repeatable approach as exemplified by the IEEE definition:

> Software engineering is the application of a systematic, disciplined, quantifiable approach to development, operation, and maintenance of software; that is, the application of engineering to software.[5]

This systematic, disciplined, and quantifiable approach to software development has proved to be very effective at developing safety critical systems. The team that writes the software for the space shuttle, for example, used this approach and has managed to achieve an admirable defect rate.

> The last three versions of the program—each 420,000 lines long— had just one error each. The last 11 versions of this software had a total of 17 errors. Commercial programs of equivalent complexity would have 5,000 errors.[6]

In the process, however, other process constraints had to be relaxed.

> Money is not the critical constraint: The group's $35 million per year budget is a trivial slice of the NASA pie, but on a dollars-per-line basis, it makes the group among the nation's most expensive software organizations.[7]

This is an appropriate engineering trade-off. When lives are at stake, it makes sense to use whatever resources are needed to ensure that nothing goes wrong. But what about software development when the consequence of error is lower?

---

5. *IEEE Standard Computer Dictionary*, ISBN 1-55937-079-3, IEEE, 1990.

6. "They Write the Right Stuff," *Fast Company*, http://www.fastcompany.com/online/06/writestuff.html.

7. "They Write the Right Stuff."

Good Enough Software—Software Engineering for the Masses

For some software, rapid development of feature-rich applications is what matters. The idea is that users will put up with errors in programs because they have so many useful features that are unobtainable elsewhere. As Edward Yourdon[8] put it, "I'm going to deliver a system to you in six months that will have 5,000 bugs in it—and you're going to be *very* happy!"

Good enough software is a logical extension of the ideas of software engineering. It represents the engineering trade-off between resources, schedule, features, and defects. The space shuttle software is safety-critical, so it has to minimize defects, accepting the resulting schedule and resource demands. Commercial shrink-wrapped applications like word processors and Web browsers need lots of features that must be developed quickly. Resources are constrained by the need to make a profit, so the engineering trade-off is made to shrink the schedule by spending less time removing known defects. The idea is that for some kinds of known defects, it is not economic to take the time to remove them.

Is Software Engineering a Good Choice for Your Project?

Systems engineering projects that involve the development of new hardware and software are a natural fit for software engineering. Many defense and aerospace projects fit within this category. When I'm a passenger in a "fly by wire" aircraft, I want to know that a *systematic, disciplined, and quantifiable approach* was taken to the development and verification of the flight control software. After all, it would not be very comforting to know that the software "was developed by the lowest bidder."

If your organization develops large, shrink-wrapped consumer software applications and is good at making appropriate engineering trade-offs, you might be able to use the *good enough software*

---

8. Yourdon, Edward, *Rise and Resurrection of the American Programmer*, Prentice-Hall, 1996.

approach. The key to success with this type of software engineering is volume. You need to be selling millions of units in a competitive market where customers buy on the basis of reviews and marketing rather than on detailed, side-by-side comparisons of products.

In all other cases, you should be looking for alternatives to software engineering.

Chapter 2

The Problems with Software Engineering

The biggest problem with software engineering is the assumption that a *systematic, disciplined, and quantifiable approach* is the only possible approach. By imposing the mechanical engineering metaphor on software development, it stops us from seeing alternatives. Classic examples of this problem are the software engineering concepts of "defect potential" and "defect removal efficiency":

> **Defect potential:** *the total universe of errors or bugs that might be expected in a software project*

> **Defect removal efficiency:** *the percentage of potential defects eliminated prior to releasing a software project to customers.*[9]

This mechanical view omits the fact that *better developers make far fewer mistakes and are much better at finding defects.* Software engineering makes us forget that *what really matters on a project is the skill, knowledge, and experience of the individual software developers.*

In a landmark field study of large software engineering projects, the importance and contribution of exceptional designers as individuals was readily apparent:

---

9. Capers, Jones, *Software Quality*, ITP, 1997, p.331–332.

> *Many projects had one or two people, usually senior systems engineers, who assumed prime responsibility for designing the system. On about one-third of the projects we studied, one of the individuals had remarkable control over the project direction and outcome and, in some cases, was described by others as the person who "saved" the system. Since their superior application domain knowledge contrasted with that of their development colleagues, truly exceptional designers stood out in this study, as they have elsewhere, as a scarce project resource.[10]*

The field study went on to note that

> *conventional wisdom on software development often argues that no software project should rely on the performance of key individuals. The experience of many successful large projects, however, indicates why this is more troublesome in theory than in practice. An exceptional designer represents a crucial depth and integration of knowledge domains that are arduous to obtain through a group design process.[11]*

In the search for the engineering nirvana of a *systematic, disciplined, and quantifiable approach,* we have confused ourselves. We should not be talking about the *defect potential of a project;* we should be talking about the *defect potential of a developer.*

The idea is simple. An *exceptional designer* will make fewer mistakes than his development colleagues, will have a lower *defect potential,* and will have a higher *defect removal efficiency.* Fred Brooks states this really well:

> *. . . [o]ne wants the system to be built by as few minds as possible. Indeed, most experience with large programming systems shows that the brute-force approach is costly, slow, inefficient and produces systems that are not conceptually integrated. . . . The conclusion is simple: If a 200-man project has 25 managers who are the most competent and experienced programmers, fire the 175 troops and put the managers back to programming.[12]*

The key problem with software engineering is that it lets us forget about the people doing the software development. The implicit

---

10. Curtis, Bill, Herb Krasner, and Neil Iscoe, "A Field Study of the Software Design Process for Large Systems," *Communications of the ACM,* November 1988, pp. 1268–1287, p. 1271.

11. Curtis, "A Field Study of the Software Design Process for Large Systems," p. 1272.

12. Brooks, *The Mythical Man-Month,* p. 130.

promise of software engineering is that if we can just define a systematic, quantified process, anyone can be successful at software development. This idea is wrong. As the field study showed, even with a process, exceptional developers are vital to the success of projects. We need to focus our attention on how we nurture software developers so that they, too, can excel. As part of doing that, we need to question what we mean by a systematic software development process.

Can Software Development Be Made Systematic and Quantified?

Is achieving a defined and repeatable process actually desirable in software development? The team that created the SCRUM[13] software development process states the following:

> If a process can be fully defined, with all things known about it so that it can be designed and run repeatably with predictable results, it is known as a defined process, and it can be subjected to automation. If all things about a process aren't fully known—only what generally happens when you mix these inputs and what to measure and control to get the desired output—these are called empirical processes.[14]

Under this definition, *software development is not a defined process*. At best, all we can hope to achieve is an empirical process. The reason is that *the sources of all software requirements are people*. There is no way to automate requirements elicitation; rather, people must talk to each other so that the software team can learn what the users really need the application to do. At the same time, the users are learning the technical constraints and costs and then use that knowledge to adjust the feature set that they ask for.

Once the software team has learned what the user needs, there remains the problem of documenting these requirements. To have a defined development process, we need to start with complete, unambiguous requirements. This is exceedingly hard to do. Gause

---

13. http://www.controlchaos.com/.

14. http://www.controlchaos.com/ie.htm.

and Weinberg illustrate this problem well[15] by showing some of the possible interpretations of "Mary had a little lamb." By emphasizing different words or combinations of words, a completely new meaning can be generated.

> <u>Mary</u> had a little lamb. *It was Mary's lamb, not John's.*
>
> Mary <u>had</u> a little lamb. *She doesn't have it any longer.*
>
> Mary had <u>a</u> little lamb. *She had only one lamb; other people had more.*
>
> Mary had a <u>little</u> lamb. *It really was surprisingly small.*
>
> Mary had a little <u>lamb</u>. *She didn't have the curried chicken that everyone else had.*

It is practically impossible to be precise and unambiguous in English (or in any other language, for that matter). Requirements elicitation is a "high-touch" activity, and we want to make sure that developers keep on talking to their users because we cannot afford the mistakes that could arise from alternative interpretations of a written requirements document. You don't want a defined requirements capture process.

But Surely We Can Automate Some Parts of Software Development, Right?

Of course we can. But we can automate only defined processes—not those that involve rich interactions between people. Many useful software development tools that automate small, well-defined parts of the software development process exist. Configuration management and build tools make it possible to convert automatically programs written in high-level programming languages into the appropriate low-level machine code. We can do this because we can precisely define the conversion process.

We need to remember that most parts of software development that can be automated have already been automated. We, therefore, already have most of the tools we need for software development—what is missing is the skill and ability to use the existing tools. Consider the build tools. Most commercial software development projects I visit do not have an automated build process that can

---

15. Gause, Don, and Gerald Weinberg, *Understanding Requirements Quality Before Design*, Dorset House, 1989.

run unattended and e-mail any build failures to key developers. Projects that have this ability are at a great advantage. Whenever the master source code is changed, the application is built and regression tests run to ensure that the change has not broken anything. I cannot imagine working on a project without this kind of safety net.

As we automate successive parts of the software development puzzle, we find that the complexity and difficulty don't go away, but simply move around like a bubble under a carpet. Because we can have a systematic approach only to what is well known and understood, software engineering has focused our attention on the mechanical parts of software development and, in the process, devalued and deemphasized the rest. So, we have a lot of technology to deal with—optimization as well as compilers and interpreters to allow us to program in high-level languages instead of assembler or machine code, but practically nothing to help us design what the user needs and even less on how to find out what the user really needs.

The Hazards of the Good Enough Software Approach

Is software more critical to your business and yet becoming bloated and buggier? I can remember the days when a word processor fitted on a single floppy; now it seems that we will soon be seeing applications that won't fit on a single CD. For many shrink-wrapped applications, each release seems to require that you buy more memory or get a faster machine. And most of the new features don't work very well.

Does your software look nicer but prove much harder to use? Sometimes it seems as if the developers spent so much time getting the application to look nice that they forgot that other people actually have to use the application.

Are projects taking longer and delivering less than promised? Vaporware is one of the wonderful terms that the software industry has added to our language. The first few releases may be out quickly, but each enhancement takes increasingly longer to appear as the software grows in complexity. Reducing the defect count to an acceptable level also takes longer as complexity grows.

Do the developers seem unresponsive to your needs when you report a defect? That is the reality of the engineering trade-off in the good enough software approach. If a defect affects only a small proportion of the possible users, it won't make economic sense to fix the problem. If you are lucky, a workaround will be found.

The good enough software approach is hazardous because it perpetuates the myth that defects are inevitable. The defects exist because of the crazy way that the software is developed. Good enough software is characterized by a coding frenzy to get an application "feature complete," followed by an indeterminate period of testing and debugging. Small wonder that the cost of removing all of the defects is considered excessive, because most features have probably been implemented on top of existing errors. By separating the activities of coding and testing into distinct phases, the good enough software approach guarantees that the application will contain lots of defects.

Shipping software with known bugs is not a good idea. Even if all of the known serious or critical bugs are fixed, shipping with known bugs sends the wrong message. It says that you don't know how to fix the mistakes you have made in the software. Even worse, it suggests that you do not care about creating quality, reliable software.[16] Ask any car dealership about how having a reputation for low reliability affects sales as soon as a high-reliability alternative becomes available.

What Is the Alternative to Software Engineering?

There is not just one alternative to software engineering. There are many different approaches that have been tried over the years for the development of software. Before we can approach these issues, we must first break free of the mechanical software engineering metaphor and understand the true nature of software development.

---

16. Minasi, Mark, *The Software Conspiracy*, McGraw-Hill, 2000.

Chapter 3

Understanding Software Development

Is software development a mechanical task? I don't think so. Typing the code has never been the rate-limiting step, so physical analogies are not really appropriate. Although we are familiar with simple mechanical analogies, these analogies cause us to make mistakes. The really common one is the old mathematical school puzzle: If two people can dig a hole in four days, how long will it take four people?

The standard textbook answer to this puzzle is two days, but the simple mathematical world rarely corresponds to reality. Before we can say whether adding more people is a good idea, we need to understand the problem first.

- What is the rate-limiting step in the process? (Yes, we can dig faster, but we are limited by how fast we can pump the ground water out of the hole.)

- What are the resource limits? (More people would be nice, but we have only one backhoe.)

- What are the scheduling constraints? (The customer said the job had to start today and these workers were the only people we could find on such short notice.)

- Is the problem decomposable? (The hole is so small that only one person can work at a time.)

- Is there any point in finishing sooner? (The next tasks are already scheduled, and finishing earlier would just mean that the hole has longer to deteriorate before we pour the concrete.)

- Are people interchangeable? (Training a good backhoe operator takes a while.)

Although we would fail the math quiz, by applying what we know about digging, we have a better chance of predicting the real effect of adding two extra people to this job. This is the real problem with the software engineering metaphor. We have a very simplified idea of what engineering means but lack the deep knowledge that is required to utilize the metaphor effectively.

To be useful as a metaphor, a concept has to be well known (if not well understood) by the people who will be using it. This reason explains why the "Mythical Man-Month"[17] problem still exists. It seems so simple. If a software project is late, just add more people and it will be done sooner. Projects are *still* making this mistake more than 25 years after Fred Brooks pointed out that this simple idea is a great way to make the project even later! Crazy. It's as if we do not really understand the nature of software development.

Software as Capital

From an economic perspective, software is embodied intellectual capital.[18] But software is not the same kind of capital goods as, for example, a car. Software is the equivalent of *the design for the car*. We need to be clear on this distinction. In the mechanical world, designing something and then producing goods based on that design are two distinct activities. Designing a new car takes several years, and, when the design is complete, factories have to be retooled to produce the new car. As the economist Howard Baetjer puts it:

> *The designing of capital, the developing of the capital structure, is a social learning process whereby knowledge is embodied in usable form.*

---

17. Brooks, *The Mythical Man-Month*.

18. Baetjer, Howard, Jr., *Software as Capital*, IEEE Computer Society Press, 1998.

What the design team has learned about automotive engineering, the needs of the marketplace, color, ergonomics, paint, and aerodynamics is converted into designs, tools, and machines. If they do a good job, factories full of relatively unskilled workers can produce hundreds of new cars every day. All of the unknowns are worked out during the design process, so that the actual production of the cars is a defined, well-known, repeatable process.

Software development is all about the unknown. The production process for software is trivially easy—just copy a disk or CD. The software engineering metaphor fails because we understand *production, a mechanical task,* much better than we understand *design, an intellectual task.*

The process of developing software involves taking both explicit and tacit knowledge and embodying it in software. Howard Baetjer sees the key challenge of software development as coordinating distributed learning and the key limitation as "our sheer ability to understand what it is we are trying to do."

This idea ties in with the observations made in the field study mentioned in Chapter 2. *Exceptional designers stood out because of their superior application domain knowledge.* That study also went on to say

> . . . [d]eveloping large software systems must be treated, at least in part, as a learning, communication, and negotiation process. Much early activity on a project involved learning about the application and its environment. . . . Further, as the project progressed they had to learn about design and implementation decisions being made on other parts of the system in order to ensure the integration of their components. Characteristically, customers also underwent a learning process as the project team explained the implications of their requirements. This learning process was a major source of requirements fluctuation.[19]

Support for this idea also comes from the hacker[20] belief that "Information wants to be free." Free access to the source code means that developers can learn from one another and build on one another's successes. The idea started from the habit of leaving all

---

19. Curtis, "A Field Study of the Software Design Process for Large Systems," p. 1283–1283.

20. Levy, *Hackers.*

paper tapes by the machine so that whoever was using the machine had access to the best possible tools. Each programmer used and improved these common tools to make programming easier. Proprietary source code was seen as an insult, because it was locked away and other programmers could not learn from it. These early hackers understood that learning from each other was an essential part of software development.

Software Development Requires Teamwork

Software development is not a solo, intellectual task. Rather, it is a collaborative, social task that requires lots of communication. Developers rarely write software purely for their own use, so even the smallest project involves at least two people—the developer and the user. To understand what the user needs, there has to be communication between the developer and the user. Learning how to collaborate effectively to deliver software is one of the key challenges new developers face when they start working on real projects.

This was less true in the early days of software development, when the main challenge involved programming the computer. As developers slowly created better ways of programming, the challenge shifted toward the design activities. For many modern projects, the main challenges lie in the requirements activities and how they interact with the design of the software.

Does the Division of Labor Work for Software Development?

In identifying three activities in software development (requirements, design, and programming), an obvious question to ask is, "Should developers specialize?" After all, the division of labor was the foundation of the Industrial Revolution. By breaking down manufacturing activities into smaller, well-defined tasks, the productivity of a group of workers can be drastically increased. Surely this approach would work for software development as well.

It seems simple, doesn't it? Have some people specialize as analysts who can work at eliciting and documenting the requirements. Have designers who take those requirements and produce specifications from which the programmers write code. Surely this strategy will be a more effective way of working.

No, it is not. The more a task is broken down into small steps, the more time is spent passing information from one person to another. A production-line approach works well for manual labor, but it fails miserably for intellectual tasks.

Software development occurs in the heads of the people on the team. By forcing people to specialize in a particular activity, delivering even a simple project requires multiple hand-offs. Each hand-off is expensive in terms of the potential for mistakes and defects. Yes, we can minimize this problem by requiring extensive documentation so as to reduce the risk of incorrect assumptions and mistakes, but this effort just adds to the project costs. As Fred Brooks pointed out, when the task is dominated by communication between the workers, adding more people slows down the project.

Software development works best when the developer has a deep understanding of the requirements, design, and source code. All of the hackers interviewed by Steven Levy did their own design and programming. Susan Lammers also noticed this when she interviewed "19 programmers who shaped the [personal] computer industry."[21] None used software engineering-style division of labor, and all had been deeply involved in both design and programming. Interestingly, they each had their own unique style of working.

One Size Does Not Fit All

Software development is intriguing because it is so variable. It is not possible to cover the massive range of software projects with a single software development process. Writing operating systems is different from writing games, and both of these jobs are completely different from writing business applications. We need to allow for this variability in the way that we develop software. As Tom DeMarco puts it:

---

21. Lammers, Susan, *Programmers at Work*, Microsoft Press, 1986.

> *As I get older and crankier, I find myself more and more exasper-*
> *ated with the great inflexible sets of rules that many companies try*
> *to pour into concrete and sanctify as methods. The idea that a single*
> *method should govern even two different projects is highly suspect:*
> *the differences between projects are much more important than the*
> *similarities.*[22]

Whenever I visit a project, I attempt to discover what factors govern how fast the project can be delivered. I am continually amazed by the sheer variety of rate-limiting steps that projects experience, including

- Agreeing on the budget for the project
- Selecting the appropriate development team, especially when using outsourcing
- Getting the requirements documented and signed off (seven years and counting)
- Getting access to the business users or decision makers
- Timely decision making by the project steering committee
- Finding good designers and programmers
- Obtaining project resources due to competition with parallel projects
- Making time for detailed work, when experienced developers are occupied supervising beginners
- Getting the technology choices approved and signed off
- Testing on the very wide variety of delivery platforms
- Getting approval from the application architecture group for the overall design concept
- Achieving consensus amongst the lead developers as to the appropriate design choices
- Scheduling design and code reviews
- Debugging and performance tuning
- Getting the project started

---

22. DeMarco, Tom, *Controlling Software Projects*, Yourdon Press, 1986.

The last one always causes me to smile, because it reminds me of Jim Highsmith's advice for improving delivery speed: *Start earlier.*[23] All of these factors have a profound influence on the development process that a project and organization can use. After all, if your organization cannot free up much time for the business users to work on the project, you would be crazy to pick a process like eXtreme Programming,[24] which requires an on-site customer.

I am not implying that eXtreme Programming is a bad process. The exact opposite is true. eXtreme Programming is a great process, because it clearly states the conditions under which it can be successful. It does not pretend to be a "one size fits all" process—it focuses on a particular set of project characteristics. I just wish that other processes were as clear about their applicability.

Finding a More Applicable Metaphor Than Software Engineering

Software engineering fails because it has very limited applicability. How can I make that claim? Simple. Most software development projects do not take a software engineering approach. Even the Software Engineering Institute realizes this fact, as can be seen in the title of an article written by Watts Humpries, "Why Don't They Practice What We Preach?"[25]

One possible answer to this question is that software engineering is not all that relevant to many projects. Software engineering was created to solve the problems of really large groups working on multiyear projects. Most modern software development, however, is done in relatively small teams.

> *Software engineering emerged 32 years ago to cope with large-scale problems, and since then it has progressed significantly. However, the demographics of software development have changed, and small groups using networked personal computers now work*

---

23. Highsmith, Jim, *Adaptive Software Development*, Dorset House, 2000.

24. Beck, Kent, *Extreme Programming Explained*, Addison-Wesley, 2000.

25. http://www.sei.cmu.edu/publications/articles/practice-preach/practice-preach.html.

on surprisingly large programs. Although programming environments have evolved to support small groups, software management methods have not.[26]

The time has come to find a more appropriate and applicable metaphor—one that addresses the social learning aspects of software development.

---

26. Laitinen, Mauri, "Scaling Down Is Hard to Do," *IEEE Software, September/ October 2000.*

Chapter 4

Finding a Better Metaphor Than Software Engineering

We need a new metaphor because we have solved most of the mechanical challenges that used to face developers. As we have moved from writing in assembler on memory-limited devices to using high-level languages, the intellectual bookkeeping challenge of deciding how to make the best use of available memory has been replaced with the challenge of clearly expressing the design intention to the rest of the team so that the system can evolve. Over time, then, the nature of the challenges facing software development projects has changed, and the expectations that we have for software are drastically different.

Our customers' expectations have also changed. Initially, they were happy with whatever printout they could get. Now, however, they expect to be able to manipulate the kind of virtual reality, three-dimensional model that is commonly used in house design. Meeting these types of challenge is typically beyond a solo developer, so commercial projects typically use small teams of developers with complimentary skills.

These changes mean that we need to start paying a lot more attention to the collaborative, intellectual aspects of software development. Indeed, for many projects, the social and cultural aspects provide the most difficulty. The stereotype of the loner, or cowboy, programmer is slowly changing as developers realize that they have to collaborate to produce really great software. Small, tightly knit teams of developers are becoming increasingly common.

To deal with these challenges, many new processes and ways of organizing software developers have been tried. Technology solutions have been suggested, giving us CASE tools that attempted to automate the programming aspects of software development. Managerial solutions have been introduced, giving us very detailed methodologies for organizing developers but providing very little guidance on how to do the tasks. Recently, solutions that pay attention to people and how they interact have been put forward, giving us ideas like eXtreme Programming.

eXtreme Programming works by paying attention to the craft of software development, to what developers and customers do on a minute-by-minute basis. Although initially this approach was seen as controversial, a key factor in the acceptance of eXtreme Programming by developers is that it fits the way that humans like to work. More than anything else, it supports software development as a social process. It takes what has been seen as a purely intellectual challenge and transforms it into a conversation. Rather than reading documents, developers talk to the users and one another, and they pair up for producing all production code. eXtreme Programming is interesting because it has practices in place for ensuring that the people on the project work together as a team. By forcing developers to communicate about the system they are building, eXtreme Programming is re-creating a craft studio where everyone learns from each other.

The Craft of Software Development

In many ways, eXtreme Programming has rekindled the debate about whether software development is science, engineering, or art. By insisting on testable requirements, it supports the science and engineering aspects. But by designing by talking about the system metaphor, it also supports the argument that software development is an art.

A recurring theme among software developers has been the idea that software development is really a craft. Although this idea has been underrepresented in books (*The Pragmatic Programmer,*[27] *The Practice of Programming,*[28] and *The Craft of Software Testing,*[29] being notable exceptions), the craft concept really resonates with developers. Similarly, Paul MacCready's talk at OOPSLA 1998[30] drew loud applause when he talked about the actual process that was used to build the human-powered aircraft that won the Kramer Prize.

At one point MacCready mentioned how the blueprints for the *Gossamer Condor* were created after the team had won the Kramer Prize. The Smithsonian Institution wanted detailed engineering drawings, and MacCready talked about how long it took to create the drawing for one part that they had just bent to fit. What design drawings they had were scratched in the dust on the ground, because "they got paid for flying a figure eight, not drawing blueprints." This idea really resonated with developers, who much prefer to write the software rather than write the design documents for the software.

MacCready also pointed out that his team perfected the *Gossamer Condor* by flying it and crashing it. Parts that broke were strengthened; parts that didn't break were made lighter and weaker. Through a very rapid crash-and-fix cycle the team managed to make the *Gossamer Condor* light enough to fly, yet strong enough not to break while being flown. As the Smithsonian Institute reports:

> One advantage of the Gossamer Condor *over previous manpowered aircraft was the facility with which it could be modified or repaired. After a crash, it could be returned to flying condition within twenty-four hours, enabling the aircraft to be tested extensively and easily modified.*[31]

---

27. Hunt, Andrew, and David Thomas, *The Pragmatic Programmer,* Addison-Wesley, 2000.

28. Kernighan, B. and R. Pike, *The Practice of Programming*, Addison-Wesley, 1999.

29. Marick, Brian, *The Craft of Software Testing*, Prentice Hall PTR, 1997.

30. "Unleashing Creativity While Still Getting the Job Done," http://www.uvc.com/videos/oo98MacCready.video.html.

31. http://www.nasm.edu/nasm/aero/aircraft/maccread_condor.htm.

MacCready's talk was inspirational for developers, because it pointed out that creating an evolvable design that can be tested is more effective than trying to create the perfect design on the drawing board.

I see software development as a creative blend of art, science, and engineering, whose purpose is to deliver effective systems. The best way I have been able to describe this idea is by talking about software craftsmanship. The software craftsmanship metaphor allows developers to acknowledge all aspects of their craft—the artistic and aesthetic aspects as well as the measurable and mechanical aspects.

Parallels with Traditional Craftsmanship

Interestingly, there are many parallels to software craftsmanship in the traditional craft of being a blacksmith. A lot of technical knowledge is needed to be effective, but that knowledge is ineffective without the practiced skill with the tools and an eye for the aesthetics of the items being produced. The intriguing part of this analogy with blacksmiths is that there are many parallels between the history of the blacksmith trade and the history of software development.

Initially, blacksmiths had to do everything for themselves. Relatively quickly, however, the extraction and smelting of iron ore were handled by other people, as was the making of charcoal. During the prehistory of software, programmers were intimately involved with the development of the hardware, but very quickly the hardware engineering and systems programming fields diverged from the field of applications development. As science and technology improved, the quality of the supplies to blacksmiths changed and (mostly) improved, and a lot of the grunt work was removed as iron became available in a range of different bar stock sizes. Similarly, some of the grunt work was taken out of applications development as machine code and assembler were replaced by COBOL and FORTRAN.

As the world of manufacturing improved, prebuilt components became available to blacksmiths, and they could purchase standard tools rather than having to make all of their own. The same shift happened in software development as operating systems became more sophisticated and standard components such as function libraries and databases became available.

As manufacturing improved further, the craft of the blacksmith nearly died out due to competition from mass-produced items. Recently, however, there has been a resurgence of interest in unique, hand-crafted items, and the craft that was nearly lost is now making a comeback. In software development, the same trends led to the prediction that programmers would soon be obsolete as software factories took over their duties. As the software engineering ideas gained strength in the mainstream, although software developers never really became comfortable with the underlying premise, most tried to adopt the industrial model of software development.

The Resurgence of the Craft of Software Development

For many years, software engineering has dominated the conversation about software development. In the background, the craft of software development was nevertheless very much alive. The early history of personal computing is a testament to individuals and small teams that made it happen.[32] Similarly, the open source and UNIX communities take a craft approach to software development. This idea was brought home when one reviewer joked that "Software engineers use Ada; craftsmen use C."

The time has come to start talking about whether the emperor is as well dressed as we are supposed to think he is. His garments definitely do not cover everything. A lot of software can be traced back to one developer or to a very small group of developers working together to produce a tool that they needed for their own use. A lot of the technology of the Web was built this way, and Perl, the Apache Web server, sendmail, and even Java started off with a very small team of developers. As the tools available to developers improve, skilled practitioners can create applications that would previously have required very large teams of developers. An example of this

---

32. Lammers, *Programmers at Work*.

idea was described by James O. Coplien in *Borland Software Craftsmanship*,[33] which documents how a very small team of developers created Quattro Pro for Windows. More than six years after the publication of that article, it is now time to start paying attention to software craftsmanship.

---

33. www.bell-labs.com/~cope/Patterns/Process/QPW/borland.html.

PART 2

Software Craftsmanship

A key failing of the software engineering metaphor is that it fails to place people at the center of the software development process. Although lots of money has been spent over the years trying to get people out of the software development process, none of the attempts has really worked. The old dreams of natural-language specifications being read by computers that then automagically create your software are just that—dreams. The only way currently to make this process work is to give the computer an extremely detailed specification in a formal language—an activity that we all know as "programming the computer."

A very big gap separates requirements specifications and design specifications, and when we forget this distinction, we may confuse ourselves into thinking that software development is easy. We do not have any tools that let us bridge the gap between requirements and design. Skilled developers are the only way to do it effectively. Finding enough skilled developers to meet the demand for new software has always been an issue. Part of the problem is that there was a hidden assumption that software development is easy, with only knowledge of the particular technology and obscure syntax being needed. Unfortunately, this isn't true. Having knowledge is not the same as having the skill and practical ability to apply that knowledge to create software applications. This is where craftsmanship comes in.

Craftsmanship has been used for centuries for the successful transmittal of skills and the development of communities of practice. For a long time, engineering relied on the craft tradition of apprenticeship. It has moved away from that idea into academic-based training programs only in the last few decades. During this transition period, the stereotypical image of education not meeting the needs of the real world was developed, not so much in the sense of Ivory Tower academics, but in the sense of mathematical models and ideas not quite matching up with reality. Academic teaching of a technical subject tends to downplay the human element. Students learn about *the requirements*, without ever taking time to think about where the requirements come from or learning the facilitation skills necessary to elicit them from the user communities. Similarly, they do not learn about the pragmatic stance that is necessary to ship the system and the cleanup work that is done afterward to enable the system to evolve.

Chapter 5

Putting People Back into Software Development

Many years ago, a really interesting change occurred in software development. That is, the software became the most expensive and important part of the system. At one time, the hardware was the most expensive part of a system, but now the cost of developing the software exceeds the cost of the hardware. This is the new reality of software development—people are the most expensive resource. Unlike the case in practically all other industries, software is becoming more, not less, labor-intensive. As the cost of computers has fallen and computers have become more pervasive, our model for developing software has not adjusted to match these new realities.

Under the software engineering paradigm, the exploding demand for software developers was met by providing short retraining programs that taught a restricted set of technical skills. Typically these courses were less than six months long and aimed to make people productive enough that they could work on projects. In parallel came repeated attempts to define Computer Aided Software Engineering (CASE) tools that would do away with the need for hordes of programmers. Both of these approaches failed.

The retraining program idea failed because it doesn't take very long to teach the syntax of a programming language. Over time, these programs either were shortened or tried to cover a wide range of technologies under the misguided notion that the syntax was all that mattered. What was missed in this effort was the real craft of software development and all of the programming lore that had built up during the 1960s and 1970s. Without this knowledge of what software development really was, projects started to repeat the classical mistakes that had been made in the past.

The vision that CASE tools would eventually eliminate the need for programmers also turned out to be a myth, because it turns out that writing the code is no longer the hardest part of software development. The reason that large projects report productivity in the range of 10 to 100 lines of code per developer-week is not that the developers are slow at writing code, but rather that it takes a lot of time to figure out what to write.

Craftsmanship Is About Getting Better at Software Development

Rather than attempt to industrialize and deskill software development, the software craftsmanship approach looks back into history to see how the problems of expensive labor and arcane skills were handled. Craftsmanship is about gaining mastery. Yes, a person can learn to perform a subset of the tasks in a relatively short time, but developing complete mastery does not happen quickly.

A related idea is that one practices a craft and that as soon a person stops practicing, her mastery fades. Hence beginners are apprenticed to a craft, because people cannot afford to take time away from their craft to teach others.

In traditional crafts, apprenticeship is *situated learning*,[34] where the apprentice takes over the easy, mundane tasks and then absorbs through observation and supervised practice the tacit knowledge necessary to perform the more esoteric, arcane tasks. Each apprentice trains a successor so that he can move on to more advanced tasks. In this manner, the master craftsman has to be concerned only with teaching the most advanced skills and can focus attention on productive work.

---

34. Lave, Jean, and Etienne Wegner, *Situated Learning: Legitimate Peripheral Participation*, Cambridge University Press, 1991.

Interestingly, the idea of training your successor is frowned upon in the engineering world, as it is likely to introduce unnecessary variations from the standard process. In contrast, the craft world expects everyone to adapt the process to suit his own unique abilities and talents. What matters is the outcome, not the process by which it was achieved.

Craftsmanship Encourages Developers to Write Great Software

Software craftsmanship makes us consider the people doing software development. What makes exceptional developers exceptional? What does mastery of software development look like? What lessons can we learn from experienced developers?

In the 1970s and early 1980s, a wealth of books that attempted to capture the experience and knowledge of working programmers was published. Examples include the early works of Gerald Weinberg (*PL/I Programming, A Manual of Style*, and *The Psychology of Computer Programming*), Henry Ledgard's *Programming Proverbs* books, and Jon Bentley's *Programming Pearls*. This practice of capturing tradition has been revived with the reissuing of many classic books like *Programming Pearls* and *The Psychology of Computer Programming*. Indeed, Hunt and Thomas with their book, *The Pragmatic Programmer*, have brought the ideas up-to-date. All of these books focus on the people who do software development and their attitudes and skills. *The Pragmatic Programmer* says it best: "Programming is a craft."

A Call to Arms

This book is a call to arms: *We must insist that developers really know their craft before we trust them to create systems for us or with us.* Whether you are a user, manager, or developer, it doesn't make sense to trust an inexperienced software developer. This is why we focus on software craftsmanship rather than on software engineering. The best processes in the world will not save a project from failure if the people involved do not have the necessary skills to execute the process; conversely, really good developers can make any process work.[35]

What matters is that the people working in software development be skilled practitioners of their craft and that they are continually working to hone and improve their skills.

---

35. I am indebted to Jim Highsmith for the clarity with which he expresses the distinction between having a process and having the skills to perform that process.

Chapter 6

Craftsmanship Is the Opposite of Licensing

Software craftsmanship is about getting the job done. Craftsmen build their reputations based on the quality of what they deliver to their customers, not on the processes they use or the ways in which they market themselves. Software craftsmen build their reputations based on the applications and systems that they successfully deliver to satisfied users and customers. This idea is the exact opposite of the concept of interchangeable, licensed software engineers.

Craftsmanship Is Personal

People choose craftsmen based on personal recommendations. In this regard, software craftsmanship is the exact opposite of software engineering. It does not offer an impersonalized certification or licensing of developers, but rather treats each person as an individual with unique abilities and strengths.

Although certification through impersonal certifying organizations claims to improve quality, no studies to back up this assertion exist. Claims that good developers can pass the certification exams are made, but the hidden implication that *passing the exam means you are a good developer* is really the classical problem of *confusing correlation with causality.* The fact that a developer has passed a certification exam says nothing about that person's ability to develop a useful application, only that she has learned how to pass the exam.

Peer Recognition and Recommendations Are the Route to Better Software

Software craftsmanship is different. When one developer recommends another developer, he is putting his own reputation on the line. This scenario is a whole lot different than an organization saying that "This developer passed the certification exams." The certifying organization has nothing at stake.

By making it personal, software craftsmanship guarantees that recommendations are never made lightly. This kind of peer recommendations means that everyone involved is constantly striving to improve and to become better developers.

It also gives users, customers, and managers better information. Rather than just being told that the person is a "certified Web developer," they will be told the real story—how the person actually works and how his projects turn out. Sometimes the answer may be a more diplomatic "I don't know enough about the developer's work to comment either way," but that in itself is enough information on which to base a decision.

Certifying organizations cannot provide this kind of information. Their lawyers could not risk that level of exposure to lawsuits from developers who have been maligned. Also, they could not risk it because the organization could not possibly have the necessary depth of knowledge about all of the developers whom it has certified.

At a peer level, though, it works. Any developer could name a few people with whom they have worked in the past and with whom they would jump at the chance of working again. Chances are, the same developers could also name a few people who are the kiss of death to any project. Obviously, a developer would be unlikely to give you the names of these people, but these aren't the names you want anyway. You want the names of the dream team, and these are the names any developer can give you without any fear of reprisal.

Licensing Is an Illusion

Licensing has the same traps and pitfalls as certification. True, it does look at more than just technical knowledge, but it fails because it claims to make an objective measurement of a software developer. The licensing idea claims that a core "body of knowledge" that all software professionals need to know exists. Defining what is "core knowledge" for software development is exceedingly difficult because the field is so diverse. Indeed, the ACM withdrew from a licensing effort because of problems in defining the Software Engineering Body of Knowledge (SWEBOK).

> The SWEBOK effort, which specifically excludes from the body of knowledge the special knowledge required for most safety-critical systems (such as real-time software engineering techniques), will have little relevance for safety-critical systems, and it dangerously excludes the most important knowledge required to build these systems.[36]

One problem that the ACM saw was ongoing—the rapid evolution of the field of software development. As such, it is hard to define a useful body of knowledge that covers the necessary ground but would not do anything useful to assure quality and safety.

> ACM's position is that our state of knowledge and practice in software engineering is too immature to warrant licensing. Moreover, Council felt licensing would be ineffective in providing assurances about software quality and reliability.[37]

Licensing is also inappropriate for application development because the necessary preconditions are not in place. Unlike in civil engineering, where a project can be shut down by a building inspector who determines that some work does not meet "the building code," it's practically impossible to shut a software project down due to shoddy work. The quality officer for a safety-critical systems project could shut down development, but no equivalent person in applications development has the authority or power to stop a project for shoddy work.

---

36. *Software Engineering Body of Knowledge,* http://www.acm.org/serving/se_policy/selep_main.html.

37. *Software Engineering Body of Knowledge.*

In a way, software development is more akin to the problems unearthed by the *Challenger* disaster inquiry.[38] Potential problems were known beforehand, and some engineers raised concerns about the potential risk to the safety of the fatal flight, but managers overruled them because of pressures to provide an on-schedule launch. They did not want to face the public relations nightmare of yet another delay to the widely advertised launch of the *Challenger.* The last line of Feynman's report is particularly telling: "For a successful technology, reality must take precedence over public relations, for nature cannot be fooled."

Licensing Is an Attempt to Solve the Wrong Problem

Licensing works for engineering because one licensed engineer can certify that something using accepted best practices has been built. The same is not possible with software. Certification can be applied to buildings and other mechanical structures because they involve standard materials and designs with well-known properties. They are also a lot less complex than software. Most engineering designs have very few parts. For example, cars typically have fewer than 15,000 parts and fewer than 5,000 unique part numbers.[39] By comparison, this book contains about 50,000 words, and the space shuttle software contains approximately 420,000 lines of code.

Cars are interesting because they are so complex that it is not cost-effective to have licensed engineers certify that they are built correctly. As the J.D. Power and Associates 2000 Vehicle Dependability Study[40] reported, even the best cars average more than two defects per vehicle. Some cars have serious design defects that require a complete safety recall, attesting to the fact that even the design is incorrect. Tellingly for the engineering profession, auto manufacturers rarely acknowledge a problem until they have a fix available.

In software, the problems are even harder. Even with multiple reviews and copyediting, most books contain a few typos or mistakes. Now imagine the problem that a licensed software engineer

---

38. "Minority Report to the Space Shuttle *Challenger* Inquiry." In Richard P. Feynman, *The Pleasure of Finding Things Out*, Perseus Books, 1999.

39. "BMW's 3-Series: Developing a Tradition," www.business.auburn.edu/~boulton/BMW_case.PDF.

40. http://www.jdpower.com/global/jdpaawards/releases/110200.html.

would face when asked to sign off on the space shuttle software. An individual could not sign it off as correct. Even if a person spent an entire career at that one task, she could never sign it off as correct because the software is too large and complex for any one individual to be able to guarantee that there are no mistakes. *The concept of a single, responsible engineer signing off the complete work is not feasible for software.*

The key problem is that *licensing assumes that it is possible to inspect quality into a product.* This approach is the wrong way to improve quality, and even the manufacturing world has shifted away from this concept.[41] As quality pioneer W. Edwards Deming stated, one of the key responsibilities of management is to

> *cease dependence on mass inspection and testing: much better to improve the process in the first place so you don't produce so many defective items, or none at all.*

Craftsmanship is a better option, because we do not have to put in lots of defects and then spend money removing them again. We can all benefit from this reduction in wasted time, money, and effort.

Craftsmanship Focuses on the Individual

My biggest objection to the idea of licensing software engineers is that it comes from scarcity. Steve McConnell, writing about "creating a true profession of software engineering,"[42] estimated that only 5% to 10% of current software developers would get licensed as professional software engineers.

Why waste all that other talent? If licensing is an essential part of all high-quality software development, then we should strive to bring all developers up to that level.

On the other hand, if licensing is relevant only for safety-critical and mass-market shrink-wrapped software, as McConnell suggests, why distort all of software development for a small niche activity?

---

41. Delavigne, K., and J. D. Robertson, *Deming's Profound Changes*, Prentice-Hall, 1994, p. 266.

42. McConnell, Steve, *After the Goldrush*, Microsoft Press, 1999.

We need instead to focus attention on how software developers get to become good developers.

The Problem of Software Development Is Abundance, Not Scarcity

There is no shortage of people who can develop software. As anyone who has ever placed an advertisement seeking a software developer will tell you, any marginally attractive job gets a flood of responses. There is an abundance of developers. We do, however, have a shortage of good developers with specific skill sets, and it is a lot of work to wade through all of the applications.

The idea of using certification or licensing to cut down the number of applicants to a manageable level is crazy. It simply encourages people to collect the appropriate bits of paper. Consider the number of jobs for which a university degree is mandatory. Guess what has happened? The demand for degrees went up, and there are now more places granting university degrees. Fundamentally, though, nothing has really changed. Now all of the applicants have degrees, so we have to find another mechanism for filtering them. Some may suggest that applicants with degrees are, on the whole, better developers, but that is probably just an effect of four more years of study. If a person became an apprentice to a great developer instead of studying for a degree, maybe the outcome would be even better.

Personal reputation and personal recommendations are the alternatives that software craftsmanship provides. You could call this the "Hollywood model," because it is close to the model used in the film industry. Directors and producers work with people they know, either personally or through their reputation. Failing that, they ask people they trust for recommendations, and then they closely examine the portfolio of the candidates.

In part, the Hollywood model works because the credentials of everyone in the film industry are public. The long list of credits at the end of a film are there for everyone to see. If a director sees or hears something that he likes in a film, it's easy enough to get in touch with the creator.

In the software development world, as of 2001, only the Open Source community[43] comes close to the film industry in terms of

---

43. http://www.opensource.org/.

openness about taking credit for work. If you see some Open Source code that you like, it's not hard to find the e-mail address of the author. Indeed, many software developers have built a very public reputation based on their contributions to Open Source systems and applications.

With all of these ideas in place, the stage is now set to explore the implications of software craftsmanship.

PART 3

Implications of Software Craftsmanship

Software craftsmanship is a metaphor that can radically transform the way we create and deliver software systems and that has implications for the way we develop software, manage teams, and deliver value to users. In exploring these implications, it is necessary to identify what we will have to do differently in order for these changes to occur. After all, things rarely change just because of an idea; instead, they change because we act on the idea and make decisions based on it.

Software craftsmanship will make a difference to the experience of using systems and in the process of actually getting systems written, both from the customers' and the managers' viewpoints. These areas are explored separately to highlight the major differences and changes that will have to be made.

We then turn our attention to the people actually doing the development work, the software developers. A central tenet of the craft model is that it is hard to pick up a skill just by being told about it. You actually have to practice the skill under realistic conditions and under the watchful eye of an experienced practitioner who is providing feedback. In applying the apprenticeship model to becoming a craftsman, we can draw on the experiences and cultures of other crafts. In borrowing these traditions, we need to allow for differences between software and traditional crafts and to ensure that the advances made in software engineering are not lost. We need to be like blacksmiths, using the extra tools that engineering gives us and using the knowledge gained by science to supplement what we know from practice. Above all, we need to put pride back into software development.

Craftsmanship is not a rejection of science and engineering, but rather a subtle blending of man, machine, and knowledge to create useful artifacts. This blending is the aim of craftsmanship—that is, obtaining mastery over science and engineering so that we can continually refine our craft. Ultimately, it is about humans regaining control over their environment, rather than machines dictating what is possible.

Chapter 7

How Craftsmanship Affects the Users of Systems

Crafted items are expected to work because they are the basis of the relationship between the user and the craftsman. Yes, crafted items have their own personality, but they are workable for the intended task. Even allowing for their special characteristics and personalities, crafted items are the items to which the users come back after trying the alternatives. Users trust their crafted items because they know the craftsman and can talk to that person if the need arises.

Knowing the craftsman is really important because it empowers the users to offer thanks, ask questions, and raise issues. Software developers share the human trait of liking to know that their work is appreciated and that they are making a difference. Knowing that their work is appreciated gives them the energy to deal with the questions and issues that arise. Without this kind of relatedness between developer and user, an unhealthy dynamic can arise in which communication between users and developers passes through intermediaries who act as gatekeepers and filters of the messages. Users then lose their connection with the people who are writing the software and can easily come to see the developers as unresponsive and arrogant; developers hear only about questions and problems and hence come to see their users as ungrateful, whining *lusers*[44] (pronounced *losers*).

In contrast, craftsmanship allows for a deeper sense of connection between the developers and users so that they can collaboratively create effective, productive solutions or troubleshoot the cause of an interconnected systems problem. This scenario is unlikely to happen if a developer is asked to work with a bunch of *lusers*.

Software Craftsmanship Works Because Software Is Easy to Copy

In the mechanical engineering world there are many economic arguments as to why craftsmanship is no longer feasible—primarily due to the cost of manufacturing the physical goods. The problem cited is that the craftsman's time to make the item has to be paid for by each customer. A solution to this problem is to have the goods *designed for manufacture* by automated machines, subtly altering the design so that it is cheaper and faster to manufacture. The downside is that we sometimes get assemblies that cannot be repaired, only replaced. For many manufactured goods, this trade-off is acceptable. There is, however, a quality trade-off, because manufactured items are made only in standard sizes. Items are cheap and plentiful, but they don't quite fit as well as a crafted item would. We end up trading off cost against quality. We get a cheap off-the-rack suit as opposed to an expensive, tailor-made suit that actually fits.

Different economics apply for software. The ease of making extra copies of software is a major challenge to the commercial sale of software.The initial design and development of software are very similar to the design and development of complex physical goods. Design and development are expensive and take time. The differences show up in the cost of reproduction and distribution of that design to the eventual users. Reproduction and distribution of software are easy and inexpensive. In fact, many schemes have been invented specifically to make it harder to copy software. (Copyright

---

44. Levy, *Hackers*.

laws exist to try to curtail this type of copying, but these laws exist precisely because copying is so easy.)

Software craftsmanship is a workable option because it doesn't take much investment to mass-produce software. As the *Borland Software Craftsmanship* study showed, small teams can produce great software. The challenge faced by craftsmen is that traditionally they have dealt with very small markets, leaving the mass market to manufacturers.

The Challenge of the Mass Market

For some standard software applications, such as word processors, the cost of design and development of *shrink-wrapped* (off-the-rack) software can be spread out over literally millions of copies. This fact provides an interesting challenge for software developers, because it is not feasible to interview all users to determine their needs. As a consequence, shrink-wrapped software is sold on the basis of its features. Magazine reviews regularly compare applications on this basis and send the message that "more features mean better software." These reviews also put pressure on organizations to be first with a feature or to respond quickly whenever a competitor includes a new feature in its product.[45] Unfortunately, these same reviews rarely discuss bugs, so the response from organizations has been to sell *good enough software.*

As noted in Chapter 2, good enough software is an application of software engineering ideas that trades off features, delivery schedule, and quality. Unfortunately, it has led to bloated, slow, and buggy applications. It produces software that sells, rather than software that is useful and productive in the hands of users. Each new version is larger and more feature-rich than its predecessor and contains enough incompatibilities to encourage people to upgrade whenever a new version comes out. The problem is that the users of the software are not well represented during the development process. Their voice is not really heard by the software developers.

For many users, a smaller, less feature-rich, but more robust application that remains stable over time would be a better solution. The current trend toward putting a date in the name of the software product and changing the file format with each release is in direct

---

45. Minasi, *The Software Conspiracy.*

opposition to the real users' needs. Organizations do this to create a demand for the latest version, but it is a losing strategy in the long run. New file formats are a massive waste of time for everyone. It is a real hassle when someone sends an unreadable file, especially when saving it in an earlier format causes subtle changes in the layout.

Of course, software developers are careful not to do this to themselves. Many programmers' text editors have remained virtually unchanged for more than 20 years. When new features are added, developers are careful not to break any existing features or change the file formats. Clearly, developers do know how to craft software for many users.

It is really a simple matter to create a robust core application that can be extended and enhanced. Using good design and careful modularization, developers have produced for themselves many tools that have lasted for many, many years. For some reason, however, they never got around to offering that type of application to their *lusers*.[46]

Craftsmen Have a Different Relationship with Their Users

Software craftsmanship stands for a different kind of relationship between developers and users. It stands for putting useful, sharp tools in the hands of the users and recognizing that over time everyone is becoming more technically astute. Yes, there will always be novices, but most fields of human endeavor call them beginners or learners, never *dummies* or *lusers*. This is why craftsmanship is so important. It reestablishes the relationship between users and developers.

Alan Cooper, a visionary software author, is a strong advocate for users in the design of software. He also has a very interesting viewpoint on how to design mass-market software:

---

46. The best part is that the software companies have managed to convince users that it is their fault. How else can we explain the *Dummies* series of books, other than that computer *lusers* think of themselves as dummies?

To create a product that must satisfy a broad audience of users, logic will tell you to make it as broad in its functionality as possible to accommodate the most people. Logic is wrong. You will have far greater success by designing for one single person.[47]

Cooper goes on to explain that in focus groups, 80% of people hated the new Dodge Ram pickup truck that Chrysler was thinking of producing. Robert Lutz, the chairman of Chrysler, went ahead with production because the other 20% loved it. The new Dodge Ram pickup truck became a best-seller. Why?

If you want to achieve a product satisfaction level of 50%, you cannot do it by making a large population 50% happy with your product. You can only accomplish it by singling out 50% of the people and striving to make them 100% happy. It goes further than that. You can create an even bigger success by targeting 10% of your market and working to make them 100% ecstatic. It might seem counterintuitive, but designing for a single user is the most effective way to satisfy a broad audience.[48]

Software craftsmen can use this idea to challenge the good enough software approach. Develop a close working relationship with a small number of users, and then create the best possible application for these users. Make them ecstatic. Then the application will be ready for release to the mass market.

But Remember, the Buyer Might Not Be the User

Software craftsmen must always remember to design for the user. Designing for the buyer is a great way to create *shelfware*—software that is bought but just sits unused on the shelf. Shelfware looks good during the demonstration, but when you try to use it on a daily basis, *it just gets in the way*. Life is easier if you don't use the software at all.

The way out of this user–buyer dilemma is to realize that users nearly always find a way to get what they really need. If it's really great software that matches exactly what the users need, it will get on the approved products list really fast.

---

47. Cooper, Alan, *The Inmates Are Running the Asylum*, SAMS, 1999, p. 124.

48. Cooper, *The Inmates Are Running the Asylum*, p. 125–126.

Great Software Deserves to Be Signed

Software craftsmanship is all about putting responsibility and pride back into the software development process. As Hunt and Thomas[49] state, we need to start "signing our work" again, just as other craftsmen do. Signing our work creates a connection between the developer and the user. The user can see who created the software and how to get in touch with that person. Companies are starting to realize that large, faceless organizations are not what customers want. For that reason, many marketers are trying to put faces to their organizations by image advertising, in which an actor pretends to be a caring employee of the corporation. Software craftsmanship says that we do not need to fake it. We can let people know who actually created the software (indeed, many computer games roll the credits at the end, just as a movie does).

By signing our work as developers, we state our willingness to stand behind our creations and be held responsible for problems that arise in use. This stance is profoundly different than that taken by current software licenses, which basically seem to say "Sold as is; we accept no responsibility for this software." Yes, we might need some protection in place against outrageous claims for the effects of mistakes, but that is very different from disclaiming responsibility and then charging users when they ask questions or try to report a bug.

Signing Our Work Changes Things

Knowing that we are going to be standing behind our product forces us to pay attention to details. When I first started working on the maintenance of a payroll system in the early 1980s, we paid special attention whenever we changed the system. In that job, the payroll manager said, "I'm not going to be the one to explain to 7,000 people why they didn't get paid on Thursday." By putting the responsibility back on the developers, the payroll manager created a situation in which developers learned to pay attention and be really careful. We knew that we were not being threatened. It was just a natural consequence of our undertaking responsibility for the payroll system.

---

49. Hunt, *The Pragmatic Programmer*.

Craftsmen Are Held Accountable for Their Work

Some people in the software field are uncomfortable with the idea of being held accountable for their actions and mistakes. Tough. It is just part of building trust between developers and users. Developers gain respect as they build a reputation by delivering solid applications that work and by how they handle any mistakes that occur. This idea is the basis of respect in all fields of endeavor—the knowledge that, if a mistake is made, adults hold themselves accountable and responsible for the ensuing consequences.

True, not everyone is ready for that type of responsibility. In that case, the person should work in an area where the consequences of error are less severe. Rather than work on medical devices or other life-critical systems where developers must really pay attention to detail, the individual should work instead on things like *brochureware* Web sites, where the consequence of error is much less significant.

Craftsmen Need Demanding Users

Users need to stop accepting bad software. Good enough software sells because users are willing to use it. To get better software, we must start demanding better software. Software craftsmanship can provide better software, but it will happen in the mass market only when users start to vote with their wallets.

Users Will Benefit from Smaller, More Robust Applications

Moving toward software craftsmanship gives users applications that contain fewer, but more robust features. The features provided will be ones that they actually need and use. Users benefit because smaller applications are easier to learn and they run faster.

These applications will evolve and improve over time, but with a solid base that will allow older versions to coexist with newer versions. Unused features will be removed so that the software doesn't just continue to grow forever. As long as the older versions remain available, removing a feature does not cause problems. Instead, users will simply choose the version they want to use based on the features they need. When a good relationship exists between the developers and users, it is unlikely that developers would remove the wrong feature. But if they did, it would not be very hard to put it back in. Users benefit from these long-lived, stable applications because they can become proficient and skilled at using the application. In addition, a knowledgeable user community can build up around the application, providing assistance to newcomers.

Software Craftsmanship Leads to Collaborative Development

The key difference with software craftsmanship is that developers and users will understand one another better and can assist each other in making the necessary trade-offs. Sometimes hard choices need to be made, but these decisions are much easier when an underlying relationship of trust and respect exists.

Chapter 8

Customers Have a Different Relationship with Craftsmen

Customers who are paying developers to create software have to stop accepting *rubbish*. The old saying from Dijkstra, "Testing cannot prove the absence of bugs," can no longer be used as an excuse for not doing a good job. Theoretically, the statement is true. In practice, however, it is possible to come really close in that any remaining errors in the software do not affect operation of the system.

Part of the key to getting error-free software was covered in Chapter 7. Having developers sign their work is a fundamental part of craftsmanship because it completely changes the mindset of the people involved in the development process. It also changes the relationship between the developers and their customers: To maintain their reputation, developers will find it necessary to push back on customer demands that they cannot fulfill.

Setting Realistic Delivery Dates

The delivery date is one area that software craftsmen will push back on. In many well-publicized software project failures, such as that involving the Denver International Airport baggage handling system, the initially requested delivery date was overambitious compared with what the developers thought possible. While a company might want to play *schedule chicken*,[50] that game is too risky for a craftsman with a personal reputation to consider.

Exposing the Fallacy of Good Enough Software

Software quality is another area that software craftsmen will push back on, because of the concept of good enough software. The problem is that the good enough software stems from the infection model of software errors, the ideas that somehow *bugs infect the software* and that *the cost of removing bugs increases as we eradicate the bugs*. The idea is that it is possible to create feature-rich applications that are so valuable that the customer will forgive the mistakes that were made in creating it.

Utter garbage. *Bugs do not infect software* in the way that colds infect people. Errors are made by developers as they design and develop the software. Some errors cause faulty behavior that makes the software do something other than what it is supposed to do. The software craftsmanship view of "good enough to ship" states that "all of the faults we detected have been rectified, and although errors might remain in the system, try as we might, we cannot find any."

Shipping with known bugs is crazy. Creating high-quality, reliable software means that software craftsmen will fix all known bugs before shipping the product. There might still be hidden defects but the probability of finding them is low. Shipping software that is free of all known defects is possible for reasonable cost. The truly expensive part of software development comes in reducing the probability that hidden defects will cause problems. For safety-critical systems, the probability of hidden defects has to be extremely low, so lots of

---

50. Schedule chicken is similar to the well-known game of chicken, in which each driver drives head-on toward another and hopes that the other will "chicken out" before the crash occurs. In software development, impossible schedules are agreed to because it is hoped that someone else will have to ask for a slippage of the schedule.

time and effort have to be spent on verification. Software crafts-manship states that we can afford to develop software with a reasonably low probability of hidden defects and that, if a defect is found, it can be fixed.

In rare circumstances, it can make sense to ship an application with a known bug for which a workaround is provided while the permanent fix is being worked on. The most likely case occurs when a subtle bug shows up in final acceptance testing a few days before the application is due to go live. Software craftsmen need to let the customer make the call. Sometimes it makes sense to the customer to ship with a few minor faults because the opportunity cost of delaying is too high. The software craftsman would then work with the customer to minimize the effect of the error and to make a permanent fix as soon as possible. The economic arguments for this practice are the same as those for good enough software, but the principles of software craftsmanship mean that this case is a rare exception, not standard practice.

By paying attention to our craftsmanship, we should never get to the situation where we have to invoke the good enough software economic argument that *we know about lots of mistakes, but it is less expensive and faster for us not to bother fixing them.* Some organizations can successfully make this argument because their software development process is so bad that their *net fix rate* for bugs is negative. A negative net fix rate is best explained by the old programmers' drinking song, "Ninety-nine bugs in a program, fix one bug, now there are 100 bugs in the program."[51] In other words, the software is so bad that in attempting to fix one mistake a developer will make several more. In that case, maybe it is time to throw out the garbage and start all over again. The customer should ask really hard questions of the development team and question whether a different team or approach should be used next time.

There Is an Alternative

In the past, customers let developers get away with good enough software because they didn't think any alternative was available. But customers now have an alternative. It is possible to create full-featured,

---

51. Normally sung to the tune of "One hundred Bottles of Beer on a Wall."

high-quality, robust applications at a price that the customer can afford. Customers just have to start insisting on high-quality, robust software and choosing their developers based on their reputation for delivering that kind of software.

Stop Choosing Developers Based on the Lowest Bidder

One of Deming's famous "Fourteen Points" addressed to management:

> *End the practice of awarding business on the basis of price tag alone; instead minimize total cost in the long run.*[52]

Users are not interested in cheap software, but rather in software that works and adds value. The difference can be striking. At one company that must remain nameless, the e-commerce Web site was put together and maintained on the cheap for roughly 18 months. because of persistent problems and customer complaints, the firm finally decided to hire an experienced developer to fix the problems. The Web site went from being a major source of problems to a great business opportunity, with more than 20% of the company's sales occurring through the Web site.

Customers can get robust software just by asking for it. The simple fact of awarding work based on reputation for delivery will have a dramatic effect on the quality of software. When customers provide this incentive, developers start paying attention to building a reputation for high-quality, robust applications. With this in place, developers will start paying attention to gaining mastery of the craft of software development; it is the basis of their reputation and, their future business depends on this reputation.

Bad Clients Will Have a Hard Time Attracting Good Developers

There is a flip side to building a reputation for delivery. Software craftsmen will take the time to assess their customers. A bad client is just as deadly to a software development project as a bad development team is, possibly worse. Good clients will realize that they have made a poor choice of developers and will restart the project with a new team. Bad clients can drive even the best-run project into the ground by delaying decisions and reversing decisions at the last minute.

---

52. Delavigne, *Deming's Profound Changes*, p. 266.

Not surprisingly, software craftsmen will look carefully at the reputation of the customer before agreeing to a project. They would be crazy not to. After all, their reputation is built on a series of successful projects. The key to a successful project is putting a good team of developers together with a good customer.

Allowing Software Craftsmen to Take Credit for Their Work

To allow a developer to build a real reputation, software craftsmanship requires some changes to the relationship between developers and customers. In particular, developers must retain their moral rights (the right to claim authorship) in all of the applications they create so that other customers can find out what they have worked on. Retaining these moral rights is the key to a developer's reputation under the craftsmanship model. Rather than being known for their degrees, memberships, or certificates, the real credentials for developers consist of the applications on which they have worked.

Holding Developers Accountable for Their Work

With the right to identification as a developer of an application comes the personal responsibility for that application—both its current performance and its future extensibility. This reason explains why customers should not ask developers to sign away their moral rights, because doing so lets the developer off the hook. This is a big mistake.

Software developers need to be held accountable for their work so that they learn from their mistakes. The original developers of the e-commerce Web site mentioned earlier were never made aware of the problems that they had left behind or the opportunities that they had missed. Because they were not held accountable, they had no opportunity to learn from their mistakes. Nothing is stopping them from making the same mistakes on future projects, because they don't even know they made a mistake.

We will not get better software until we give developers feedback on how their creations work in practice.

Start Exploiting the Difference in Productivity Between Developers

Once customers have a way of identifying good, reputable developers, they can exploit the differences in developers' abilities. Software engineering is aimed at "managing hoards of 'average' programmers working on large projects that continue for years."[53] In contrast, software craftsmanship uses talented master craftsmen who work in small teams to deliver applications in less than one year.

Software craftsmanship takes this approach because using large teams is an ineffective way to deliver applications:

> *When one startup with a team of 25 developers heard that two large, established companies were starting a joint venture to enter the same space, they were worried. Then they heard that the joint venture was using a "team" of 600 developers. They were safe. With a team of 600 they would waste a month just deciding how to format the requirements documents.*[54]

Hire Small Teams of Good Developers

Rather than hiring a horde of 30 or more average programmers, customers should hire 2 or 3 master craftsmen. Pay these craftsmen as much as you would have paid the horde of average programmers.

Yes, you read that right. Great developers deserve to be paid as much as all of the people whom they replace. This decision makes economic sense because the application produced by the small team will be much better. Small teams produce better software. Fred Brooks reiterates this idea several times in *Mythical Man-Month*, as does the *Borland Software Craftsmanship* study. Time and time again, it has been demonstrated that small teams of good developers can produce great software.

So what if this choice means paying good developers ten times more than the average programmer? High pay is how we attract good people into all fields of endeavor: sports, sales, management,

---

53. *Stumm, Michael,* "A Computer Engineer's Perspective of Software Engineering." *In Proc. National Workshop on Software Engineering Education,* Toronto, Ontario, 1993.

54. Josh MacKenzie, ThoughtWorks, personal communication.

and media. Without rewards to match their ability, talented people divert their energies into other areas.

You could argue, as Ken Auer[55] did when reviewing this book, that the real problem is that we are paying too much for lightly skilled labor. Why pay the average developer $50,000 per year when his skills are not all that special? After all, it takes only three to six months of intensive coaching and training to bring a novice up to the level of an average software developer.

What Is a Great Developer Really Worth?

Probably a lot more than they are currently being paid as employees. They are worth at least five times, and perhaps ten times, what the average developer receives. Think back to the field study discussed in Chapter 2. What was the person who "saved" the project worth? What would the consequences have been if that person had been lured away to a different organization?

Great developers are probably worthy of $150,000 to $250,000 per year. Average developers are probably worth less than you are currently paying them, and it is foolish to pay college graduates with no real-world experience $40,000 to $60,000 per year.

But How Do We Know How Good a Developer Really Is?

An obvious objection to these fantastic rewards is the problem of determining how good a developer really is. To do so, we need to see what the developer has achieved in the past. The key here is that individual's reputation for delivery. We also need to adopt some of the hiring practices that depend on star talent used in other fields. Rather than conducting an hour-long interview and possibly a short test, we need to start looking at a developer's portfolio of applications. We need to talk to the applicant's colleagues, previous customers, and managers to do all of the due diligence work required for any employee who will be paid $150,000 to $250,000 per year.

---

55. CEO, founder, and master craftsman of RoleModel Software, Inc., http://www.rolemodelsoft.com/.

Sounds crazy, doesn't it? How could one developer be worth that much?

The answer is simple. Good developers make all of the difference between success and failure. Large teams taking a long time are at a high risk of failure, whereas small teams of good developers deliver quickly and have a low risk of failure. Given a choice between paying $1 million per year for a team of 20 average developers or paying $1 million per year for a team of three outstanding developers, I'd choose the small team every time. The added bonus is that the hidden overhead costs are much smaller with the smaller team—another benefit of using outstanding developers.

Of course, another side to this argument exists. With high pay come high expectations. When you are paying that much, it forces everyone to operate at an entirely new level of excellence. You don't want your expensive new hire to be idle while facilities finds her a cheap computer and then takes a few days to give her access to all of the networks and systems. No way. When you are paying more than $2 per minute, you don't want to be on hold for very long.

Measure Developers by Their Delivery

You will naturally expect your high-priced developer to deliver, and to deliver quickly. In the words of Peter Coad, you will want "Frequent, Tangible, Working Results." Incremental development and evolutionary delivery are the key to achieving this goal and allow you, as a customer, to see an early return on your expenditure. Software development then becomes just like a masters-level, open-book exam. On day 1, the professor says, "At the end of the course there will be an open-book exam. Here is the exam that you will take, and we expect you to get 100%."[56] A master craftsman is used to this kind of expectation from the customer and values the challenge.

Your task as a customer is to begin operating at the same level. Rather than sending questions and issues to be pondered by review committees, you need to empower your users to interact directly with your developers so that things can move quickly. You don't need multiple checks and balances because good developers know

---

56. This analogy is courtesy of Bud Newman, a quality assurance consultant.

what is at stake—their reputations for successful delivery of high-quality, robust applications.

Software craftsmen insist on good quality assurance reviews and customer acceptance testing of applications. They want to make sure, before anything goes live, that customers have done their part in checking for mistakes and omissions. While these reviews and tests will rarely, if ever, catch anything, they function just like the seat belt in a car. You wear it every time, without expecting an accident. It's a real shock when it catches you, and you are glad you are wearing it. If you are careless and forget to wear the seatbelt, however, you can be badly hurt.

Software craftsmen have a real interest in automated testing because of their investments in their reputations. In a way, this concept is a throwback to the practice of having *installation verification procedures* for applications. With these procedures, as soon as you installed a new version of an application, you could test that it actually worked.

One of the key goals of incremental development is to get the application running early so that it can be tested. Once it is working correctly, it is conceptually quite simple to verify that all of the old features still work and that the new features perform correctly. Automated tests are necessary, because manual verification is both labor-intensive and error-prone. The practice of automating unit testing and functional, acceptance testing has been taken to new heights by eXtreme Programming. Interested readers should check out www.JUnit.org, which is dedicated to JUnit, a unit testing tool for Java.[57]

Customers Make a Cost/Quality Trade-off When Choosing Craftsmen

The relationship between good developers and customers is different with software craftsmanship, because it is hard to rush a craftsman. You can request a set of features by a certain date, but

---

57. Versions of this unit testing framework for many other languages are available at http://www.xprogramming.com/.

because of the need to maintain a reputation for high-quality, robust applications, software craftsmen will value quality above the feature set. This preference is a natural consequence of the craftsmanship approach. In taking this approach, a customer makes a value choice, stating that having a high-quality, robust application is more valuable than feature set or delivery date. This trade-off requires a level of trust between the customer and the craftsman such that the customer gets the needed application without forcing the development team to compromise its reputation.

The way to achieve this balance is to use incremental development with evolutionary delivery. As new features are developed and validated, they can go live. Over time the released product evolves to the fully featured application, but the software craftsmanship standpoint is that it is better to have a functional, rock-solid, minimal-feature release than an unstable, buggy release with features that don't quite work properly. Software craftsmanship takes this stand because it is easier and less risky to add functionality to a solid foundation than it is to debug your way to stability after release. We have tried "debugging our way" to stability, and it gave us good enough software. The software craftsmanship approach is a better way.

This does not mean, however, that your highly paid developers will be sitting around taking forever to produce their masterpiece. Software craftsmen understand that their reputation relies on their ability to deliver value to their customers and useful functionality to their users. Just as in other high-paying fields, if the customer is not receiving value, things have to change. If the expected benefits do not appear, then it's time to find out what is going wrong and possibly time to renegotiate the package. Remember, though, that good developers know how long things take and are rarely willing to sign up for delivering the impossible. They have enough confidence to say when a task is beyond their abilities to deliver and will happily turn down impossible challenges because they realize that taking on tasks is not the issue. In the long run, what matters is delivering high-quality, robust applications.

Software Craftsmen Specialize in Different Types of Applications and Projects

Customers have control over the cost/quality trade-off by their selection of craftsmen. By choosing a craftsman who specializes in creating high-availability, mission-critical applications, a customer is defining the required quality level. Similarly, by choosing a craftsman who specializes in the rapid delivery of departmental applications, a customer is choosing a different quality level.

By defining the appropriate *mission profile*,[58] a customer chooses what is important about the application in terms of schedule, resources, features, and defects. As Highsmith defines it, in a mission profile a customer is allowed to choose one product quality dimension at which to excel and one on which to improve; the remaining two dimensions must be classified as "accept." This last classification does not mean that any result is acceptable, but that within broad limits the outcome on that dimension will be accepted, provided that the "excel" target is met.

The fact that defects are listed as a product quality dimension does not mean a return to the flawed concept of good enough software. For software craftsmanship, products are always shipped with zero known defects. Here, "defects" refers to the probability and severity of any defects that may remain hidden in the software. For safety-critical software, the probability of any hidden defects has to be exceedingly low; even if problems exist, the software should be "fail safe." For high-availability, mission-critical applications, the probability of any hidden defects should be very low, the defects must not cause data loss, and the application must be capable of being restarted with minimal loss of service. For departmental applications, the probability of hidden defects should be low, but more important, the software craftsman should be able to fix rapidly any defects that are found.

By clearly stating the mission profile, a customer sets expectations for a project and the resulting application. The customer then needs to choose software craftsmen with a reputation that matches the desired profile. In this way, both parties understand the project priorities and agree on what is expected.

Customers Have Long Term Relationships with Software Craftsmen

Overall, because developers who adopt the software craftsmanship approach accept responsibility for the applications they create,

---

58. Highsmith, *Adaptive Software Development*.

customers benefit from the long-term relationship that this implies. A long-term relationship with developers is crucial, because the best person to maintain an application is the person who developed it.

The original developers know the application really well. Whenever a problem is reported, they know where to start looking and can typically locate and fix the problem quickly. In contrast, the lowly maintenance programmer from the software engineering world is at a severe disadvantage. This employee doesn't know the application or where to start looking. Fixes take a long time because the maintenance programmer has to learn enough about the application to understand the implications of any changes made. If they fail to do this, in all probability, new defects will be introduced.

Being the Maintainer of an Application Is a High-Status Position

The Open Source community clearly understands the importance of maintenance. Developers take long-term responsibility for maintaining a project and accept the responsibility for finding a worthy successor when it is time for them to pass the application on. The fantastic stability of the core development team is one of the keys to the success of things like emacs, GNU Linux, and fetchmail, for example. I cannot think of any commercial applications that can match the emacs editor for the continued involvement of the original developer over a period of more than 25 years (and counting).[59]

The difference between the Open Source view of maintenance and the software engineering view of maintenance couldn't be more striking. Eric S. Raymond, the maintainer of fetchmail and the author of *The Cathedral and the Bazaar,* notes that the acquisition of ownership of a project through "passing the baton" from one maintainer to another is an important event:

> It is significant that in the case of major projects, such transfers of control are generally announced with some fanfare.[60]

In the Open Source community, becoming the maintainer of an application dramatically enhances your reputation. It signals that the original maintainer trusts the new maintainer to continue to

---

59. Emacs, a very extensible text editor, was created by Richard M. Stallman in 1975. See http://www.fsf.org/.

60. Raymond, Eric S., *The Cathedral and the Bazaar,* O'Reilly, 1999, p. 90.

maintain and evolve the application in a responsible manner for the good of the entire community. Such an honor is granted only to skilled developers who have made significant contributions to the application.

Contrast this idea with the software engineering view of maintenance. You get stuck in maintenance only if you are not good enough to work on new projects. After spending millions of dollars and many developer-years of effort on creating an application, the program is entrusted to the care of the lowest of the low. Crazy.

This attitude has even affected the way we speak about software through the use of the term "legacy applications." Legacy applications are the core applications that enable a business to operate, but *due to neglect are practically impossible to maintain and enhance.* I cannot think of any other fields in which we are stupid enough to entrust the care and maintenance of essential, expensive assets to the people least qualified to look after them.

Software Craftsmanship Values Long-Lived Applications

Just as in the Open Source community, a craftsman's reputation is tied to her applications. She has an incentive to keep on taking good care of her previous work. Both the customer and the developers benefit from the fact that the developers know the application really well, so any necessary enhancements and changes can be made very quickly. Customers benefit from having applications that can be modified quickly to meet changing business needs.

Customer Interests Are Aligned with the Interests of Software Craftsmen

Customers want great software. Software craftsmen want to produce great software—something of which they can be proud and on which they can base their reputation. This fundamental alignment makes for a better relationship between customers and software craftsmen. Yes, customers will pay more per developer. The payoff is that a smaller team of skilled craftsmen can handle the projects with realistic schedules and deliver high-quality, robust applications that will last for years.

Software craftsmanship gives customers what they need—namely, stable, long-lived applications rather than old-style legacy applications that cause significant disruption and trauma every few years when they have to be replaced. Software craftsmanship provides a real alternative to the world of disposable software. It is a return to the tradition of well-crafted items that lasted for years.

Chapter 9

Managing Craftsmen

Managing software craftsmen is completely different from managing software engineers. The neo-Taylorism model[61] that is used as the default management style in the Western world assumes that the knowledge of the "one best way" to do a task lies with the managers. The hired hands are just there to do what their managers tell them to do.

Although this "scientific management" may have worked for shoveling coal back in Taylor's day, it has not proved very effective in modern manufacturing industry. Sometimes the hired hands get their revenge on the system by following orders to the letter. Few managers are filled with joy when they hear that there is going to be a "work to rule." Chaos always ensures.

Sometimes workers take the old scientific management saying, "You are paid to work, not think," seriously. In one amusing incident in a car assembly plant in the 1980s, a mixup on a line that produced both Rover and Honda cars occurred. Several hundred "Ronda" cars were built when the production line got out of sequence. Rover bodies were fitted with Honda seats and trim. The resulting hybrids couldn't be sold and ended up being used as pool cars. When I drove one of these pool cars, all of the identifying logos had been removed, so they could have been Honda bodies with

---

61. Delavigne, *Deming's Profound Changes*.

Rover trim. Either way, these "Ronda" cars were a telling tribute to the power of scientific management.

Since then, even the car companies have learned their lesson. Assembly workers can now stop the production line if a problem occurs. They are now allowed to *think* as well as to work. The lesson of this tale is obvious: *Scientific management is not an appropriate way to manage software developers.*

Software Craftsmen Are Not Hired Hands

The knowledge of how to do software development lies in the heads of the craftsmen. Developers are *paid to think* while they work. Software craftsmanship is an acknowledgment of the craft and skills of the developers. Managing craftsmen is different. People master a craft because they care enough about the craft to make the effort.

Craftsmen do not need detailed instructions about what to do and when to do it. Instead, they need managers to coordinate their work with the work of the rest of the organization, schedule necessary resources, and identify applications that need to be enhanced or modified. Craftsmen do not need command and control managers, but rather managers who are skilled in facilitating the relationships between developers, users, and customers.

Good Developers Are More Valuable Than Their Managers

This notion may come to a shock to some managers, but a really good developer is more valuable to an organization than the person who manages him. Managers need to get used to the concept of managing higher-paid employees. This outcome is a natural result of abandoning the software engineering approach of using hordes of average programmers and replacing those employees with a few good developers. Managing 30 programmers is a hard task, whereas managing 3 or 4 good developers is easy.

Hierarchical organizations do not work for software development. The command and control model of scientific management is outmoded for knowledge workers. It is not relevant when the employees—not the managers—provide the knowledge, skill, and ability to create software applications.

The Actual Process of Developing Software Cannot Be Defined in Detail

The software craftsmanship approach acknowledges that the only people who really know how to do software development are the developers who are actually doing the job. Although management adds value by planning and sequencing the work, providing resources, and so forth, Taylor's "one best way" to do a task doesn't apply to software development. The Personal Software Process[62] (PSP), as defined by Watts Humphrey, is a close adherent to the ideas of Taylor, but the PSP focuses on allowing developers to improve their own skills.

Sure, PSP uses a stopwatch so that developers can time their activities, but it does not go so far as to have a time-and-motion expert break manual activities down to define the optimal sequence of mechanical actions. Taylor used slow-motion films to time actions with a resolution of hundredths of a second when trying to understand how to optimize a mechanical operation. PSP does not follow that course. Even with its emphasis on timing the various software development activities, timing to a resolution of minutes is sufficient for PSP, because it seeks only to have developers think about where they are spending their time.

Software Craftsmen Have a Different Relationship with Their Managers

The biggest change that software craftsmanship brings for management is the insistence that *managers treat developers as knowledge workers*. The knowledge of how to do the job resides in the heads of the developers, not the managers. This has profound implications for the relationship between managers and developers. The balance of power between the managers and the developers is different. Their communications have a completely different tone. Essential

---

62. Humphrey, Watts S., *A Discipline for Software Engineering*, Addison-Wesley, 1995.

skills for managers are facilitation and coaching—the days of hands-on managers who try to control everything are numbered.

This idea is not new, but getting managers to act on it will be when the real changes show up. Unfortunately, Taylor's ideas about workers persist in the software industry—namely, that unless workers are closely supervised, they will slack off and be less productive. That kind of thinking might have been appropriate in the 1910s, but now it is completely outdated.

Managing Great Developers Is a Pleasure and a Privilege

All really good software development managers know this already. They know that managing software development projects is not like managing mechanical projects. They can see the similarities that exist and use techniques from traditional project management when they apply, but they also appreciate the differences.

For a start, they know that although projects are significant, what really matters is the long-term health of the teams and applications that they manage. Healthy teams produce great software; dysfunctional teams can destroy great software. Badly written software is a drag; it slows progress and depresses the team. Sometimes a quick-and-dirty hack is necessary and expedient, but these patches have to be reworked and cleaned up once the rush is over. Most of all, good managers appreciate the value of a team that can deliver. Once they have found such a team, they will do everything in their power to keep that team intact.

Good Managers Understand the Rhythm of a Project

Good managers also know that projects and systems have a certain rhythm. Teams can push themselves to deal with external demands, but the push must be followed by a time for rebuilding reserves. "Lean and mean" may be a way of managing mechanical tasks in stable times, but optimizing for a particular set of circumstances usually reduces the adaptability of the organization. Without sufficient adaptability, external surprises have a way of throwing lean-and-mean organizations into disorganized chaos as insufficient slack to deal with the extra variability exists.

Good managers also realize that they are managing individuals and that management is about forming a special kind of relationship between people. As such, management is not a "one size fits all" approach. Rather, managers have to adjust their style to match the styles of the people with whom they are working. Good managers engage in constant conversation with the people whom they manage, and they actually manage people by interacting with them. Command and control is out; conversation is what works.

Software Craftsmen Like Creating Applications

The craft tradition has another lesson for management. Mastering any craft is a goal in itself. In traditional crafts—even those requiring physical skills and manual dexterity, such as a blacksmith—master craftsmen were often productive and participated in their craft well beyond the age of 60. It's not as if the physical demands of software development are very onerous. So where are the older software developers? It is hard to find developers with 30 or more years of experience. Sure, some exceptions exist, but most developers seem to move up into management or out into different fields. Few remain as developers for a long time.

This exodus is a real problem: We keep repeating the mistakes of the past because we lack developers who remember the mistakes made the first time around.

The Basics of Software Development Haven't Changed All That Much over the Years

By acknowledging software craftsmanship, we make it possible for good developers to continue practicing their craft for their entire career. Yes, computer technology changes quite quickly, but many of the lessons learned in the 1960s and 1970s are still relevant today. Machines are faster, memory is plentiful, and programming languages have changed, but the basics of the craft of software development remain the same: *Make sure you understand the real problem, look long and hard for a simple solution, and when you find a solution, test it on a small scale first.*

Software development is not rocket science. It relies on experience built up over years in the school of hard knocks. The current software engineering mindset of using hordes of cheap developers practically guarantees that we will continue to repeat the mistakes of the past, because no one remembers the old mistakes. With the programming horde mentality, "more people" is mistakenly equated with "more productivity," so it's obviously better to hire two inexperienced developers than it is to hire one experienced developer (even when "experienced" means "has worked with Java for more than two years"). Sorry—wrong answer. Getting good developers is much more important than getting lots of developers.

Experienced Old-timers Are a Vast, Untapped Resource

Although software development is stereotyped as something that only young people can do, this stereotype is wrong. Craftsmen get better as they gain more years of experience. Even in traditional physical crafts like blacksmithing, 70-year-old master craftsmen are sought after for the quality of their work. Old-timers are valuable in any field; their depth and breadth of experience make a massive difference in the quality of their work. Craftsmen honor the past while enthusiastically learning in the present, so that in the future they can scale even greater heights.

Managers need to demonstrate that they value years of experience by providing training in the latest technologies to their old-timers. This may cost money and take some time, but most developers pick up new technologies surprisingly quickly. It's a better option than hiring a bunch of new developers who happen to know the technology. The new hires will have to learn the business and get to know their users. In the process, they need lots of supervision and management as they slowly learn their way around the organization. In contrast, retrained developers can continue to operate with minimal supervision and management. All they might need is some coaching in the specifics of the new technology.

Ken Auer uses a multigenerational software studio approach in his company. He brings together the wisdom and experience of the old-timers with the energy and enthusiasm of the beginners:

> . . . [it] is quite amazing how the enthusiastic beginners and the discerning journeymen and craftsmen interact. In fact, there are

moments when it is not clear who is the apprentice and who is the craftsman. Over a stretch of time, however, it is rather obvious.[63]

The dynamic described here is interesting. Craftsmen learn from the apprentices, even as the apprentices learn from them. Enthusiastic beginners not only renew the craftsmen, but also challenge the craftsmen by bringing in new ideas from outside. The power of this synergy has to be felt to be believed. A well-chosen apprentice can make even a master craftsman more productive.

Managing Software Craftsmen Is Different

Traditionally, managers had to watch out for developers adding "cool" features to products, bringing them back to working on features that the customer and users actually requested. In contrast, craftsmen have a major incentive to search for simplicity, because complexity is a major source of problems in software development. The dynamic changes, then, because craftsmen take the long view about how the choices made today will affect the software over time and how that will affect their reputations over time.

Craftsmen do not create something and then disclaim responsibility for it. Managers do not have to deal with the maintenance problem, because once a craftsman creates something, it is that person's creation to look after and enhance until the developer passes it on to a worthy successor. This process works because the creator's reputation is tied up in what they create. The Open Source community is a living example of this practice, and GNU Linux and Open Source tools exemplify this idea. Once a craftsman creates an application, she looks after it until it is no longer needed and can be retired.

Craftsmanship Is Not About Planned Obsolescence

Craftsmanship is not about *planned obsolescence*, but rather encourages and values long-lived, stable applications. It is no coincidence that the GNU tools and other freeware applications are

---

63. Ken Auer, Role Model Software, Inc., personal communication.

longer-lived than the average commercial tools. This aspect of software craftsmanship, however, is one area where the craftsmanship ideas may come into conflict with traditional organization management.

Software craftsmanship does not value change for its own sake. It values slow, evolutionary change that meets real user needs. The craftsmanship exhibited by the Open Source community provides a constancy of purpose that is unmatched by large commercial software development organizations. If managers request that a new version be deliberately made incompatible with existing versions (by changing file formats, for example) to encourage users to upgrade, then that request will be in conflict with the needs of software craftsmanship.

Resolving this conflict of interests requires communication at the start of the project. By carefully explaining the mission profile of the project and the organization's expectations, the customer and manager can ensure that the craftsman understands and can support those goals. Software craftsmen who are developing a reputation for software that is upward and downward compatible would probably reject the assignment. Conversely, those who have a reputation for creating innovative, feature-rich applications would probably relish the opportunity.

Software Craftsmen Push for What They Need

Master craftsmen are experienced developers. They know what it takes to deliver great software. As such, they will be much more insistent on having access to the eventual end users during the development process. This dialog might seem impractical for some companies, but without this type of close working relationship with the users, the developer risks creating an application that does not meet the users' needs. A software craftsman knows that this kind of fiasco does not enhance her reputation. Craftsmen want and need to work with their users, and they expect managers to facilitate this relationship.

Overall, software craftsmanship makes managing software development projects much easier because fewer people are involved. Rather than dealing with hordes of average programmers, managers work with small teams of good developers. They work with craftsmen who are their equals, not a bunch of subordinates. The payoff is rapid delivery of high-quality, robust applications.

Chapter 10

Becoming a Software Craftsman

Developers have traditionally been resistant to software engineering ideas, so why should they adopt software craftsmanship? Simple. Good developers have always seen what they do as a craft and have been searching for a way to talk about what they really do. In part, their search has been hampered by the way software engineering has dominated the conversation and by the way mainstream media have subverted the use of the word "hacker." *Hacker* once meant a skilled programmer who was able to make the computer do really useful things. Today, it generally refers to someone who breaks into and subverts systems. The combined effect of these changes has been that developers have not been able to communicate effectively about the nature of software development.

Software craftsmanship provides a metaphor that allows developers to communicate what it really means to develop applications. It legitimizes what good developers have always done. This is the real payoff for developers, because talking about craftsmanship allows developers to communicate with everyone else about the arcane lore of their craft.

Software Craftsmanship Is a Rejection of Narrow Specialization

Software craftsmanship permits developers to break out of the software engineering straightjacket that denigrates the core skills of software development: programming, testing, debugging, and maintenance. When I first started working in software development, you didn't want to be *just a programmer* forever, because programmers were relegated to the lower salary levels. To progress, you had to *rise above programming* and become a *systems analyst*. The only people who were *maintenance programmers* were either new hires or people who were not good enough to become systems analysts.

Software craftsmanship rejects the narrow role specialization that software engineering forced on developers and instead *celebrates true craftsmen who can take a complete job from start to finish.* Craftsmanship requires end-to-end involvement by a developer, as it is the only way that a developer can be confident that the work created will meet the needs of their users and customers. After all, developing an application to a specification is not useful if the specification does not fully represent what the users really need.

Specialization Slows Down Development and Introduces Errors

Having the same people involved from the initial discussions through maintaining the released application reduces the possibility of misinterpretation as an application is taken from a rough initial idea into a live, running system. The software engineering approach of having analysts passing requirements off to "architects," who in turn pass designs off to the programmers, is a guaranteed recipe for mistakes and misinterpretation.

Software craftsmanship rejects the software engineering notion that it is impossible for one person to know the entire system. Instead, it celebrates virtuosity and talent. By asserting that one person can know the entire system, craftsmanship allows developers to take personal responsibility for both the successes and failures of the system.

Software Craftsmen Build Systems That Can Be Understood

Good developers rise to the challenge of creating great applications. This challenge is a hard one, but that is the essential nature of any craft. Craftsmen take pride in completion. Doing a small part of any job is easy, but mastery of a craft really shows up when we look at the entire task. Although you can be a good technician by knowing how to do a small task really well, craftsmanship shows up in the often overlooked and hidden details. In the end, it comes back to the idea of craftsmen signing their work. They sign because they stand behind their applications. They are willing to stand behind that work because they have been involved with it from when it started to when it is ready for their customer to use.

Craftsmanship Requires Dedication

The process of becoming a software craftsman is not easy because the road to mastery of anything requires dedication and time. Software craftsmanship is a mindset and an attitude, rather than a body of knowledge. As with all crafts, mastery requires an in-depth understanding of that craft, but understanding and knowledge are by themselves insufficient. The key part of adopting craftsmanship is making the personal commitment to mastery and taking the responsibility for your own work.

Mastery is not defined by a limited body of knowledge. Rather, it is defined by peer recognition of a person's reputation for delivering high-quality, robust applications. What a person knows is less important than what he can create to meet the needs of his users, especially in the face of rapidly changing technology. A master craftsman may learn a new technology from an apprentice, but it does not mean that she is no longer a master. If anything, it reinforces her mastery because it illustrates a willingness to learn from everyone. Indeed, one of the traits associated with true mastery of any craft has been humility. Master craftsmen are always willing to learn and are able to admit their own mistakes. Both of these traits are essential for software development, because things change so fast and it is so easy to make a mistake.

How Does a Person Become a Software Craftsman?

To answer this question, we can look at the old craft traditions. Schooling is insufficient and ineffective for passing on craft traditions, because it ignores the ideas of situated learning and legitimate peripheral participation[64] that have been the mainstay of the craft apprenticeship model. In the apprenticeship model, the ratio between apprentices and craftsmen is much higher than is possible between students and teachers, because the apprentices are doing useful work. Learning becomes a lifelong, useful activity, unlike schooling that has to be "gotten through" so that you "can graduate," having "learned all you need to know."

Apprenticeship Is Much More Effective Than Schooling

In the craft tradition, newcomers start as apprentices to a master craftsman. They start by contributing to the simpler tasks, and as they learn and become more skilled, they slowly graduate to larger, more complex tasks. Interestingly, although apprenticed to a master, apprentices rarely, if ever, are shown how to do anything by their master. Instead, the task of figuring out how to do things falls to the apprentice, who will ask the other apprentices for help. From whom did the other apprentices learn? The journeymen.

Journeymen are craftsmen who have finished their apprenticeships but have not yet mastered their craft. They work for master craftsmen from whom they could learn more and show the older apprentices how to do the more important and complex parts of the craft. When they have learned all they could from their original master, they know that the time has come to move on to a different master—hence the figurative and literal journey to mastery.

Journeymen Are the Key to the Craft Tradition

Traditionally, journeymen have disseminated ideas between master craftsmen. They work with different masters to gain experience and learn new techniques and ideas. As they do so, techniques learned from one master are spread to different locations. This cross-fertilization of ideas results in new ways of doing things by combining techniques and ideas.

Journeymen become master craftsmen by producing masterpieces on which can base their reputations. Master craftsmen know that

---

64. Wenger, Etienne, *Communities of Practice*, Cambridge University Press, 1998.

producing a masterpiece is just the first step in their continual journey to master and improve their craft. As part of this tradition, they accept the responsibility of taking on apprentices and involving them in their work so that they, too, can become craftsmen.

The Craft Tradition Has Endured for Centuries

How these ideas can be applied to software craftsmanship is the subject of the next three chapters. What is important to note, however, is that the craft model of apprentices, journeymen, and masters was widespread and very successful. At some point in history, every town and village had at least one blacksmith, and each blacksmith would have a few apprentices. The craft model successfully passed craft skills across the generations and through centuries of time.

From an industrialized, schooling viewpoint, apprenticeship seems to be a slow way of getting workers up to speed with a task. Craftsmanship is self-contained, however. It does not rely on an artificial separation between the craftsmen who are making useful things and the training of their eventual replacements.

Apprenticeship takes time because it focuses more on inculcating attitudes and mindset than on learning specific techniques and technologies. Apprenticeship is more than just learning the craft, it teaches the newcomer how to conduct herself in society (when she finally becomes a craftsman). It was about learning at a very deep level about what reputation means through observation of how the master goes about the craft over many years.

For software development, the difference between the industrialized software engineering view and the software craftsmanship standpoint is the difference between trained technicians and master practitioners. Trained technicians follow the book and do what you tell them to do. Master practitioners ask lots of questions and then deliver what you really need (as opposed to what you actually asked for).

Chapter 11

Mastering the Craft

Good, experienced developers who have mastered the craft of software development by shipping many different systems are the key to software craftsmanship. They are the foundations on which we can build the software craftsmanship community as a viable alternative to the programming hordes incorporated in the software engineering model. Although good, experienced people are quite rare, they do exist and can be found. Most are either independent or working for smaller companies that value their contribution.

The challenge in finding good, experienced developers lies in finding people who have already adopted the craft tradition of continual learning. We are looking for developers who, although already good, are continually striving to improve their mastery of software development. The real test, though, is not just whether they are learning more and getting better, but rather whether the people who work with them have adopted a similar attitude toward learning and improvement. Basically, we are seeking people who are demonstrably adept at all parts of software development and have work habits that we want their apprentices to adopt as well. The key question is, "Has he infected his colleagues with his enthusiasm and passion for the craft of software development?"

What Does a Master Software Craftsman Look Like?

This question is hard to answer. The skills of master craftsmen will be different because over the years they have focused on different parts of the craft. Although a true master will understand and be able to use many technologies and platforms, it is unrealistic to expect a master to know every technology. More than 200 programming languages are still actively used on projects, each of which can easily take many years to understand and appreciate fully. We can, however, expect true craftsmen to become productive quickly in any technology that is reasonably close to what they were already familiar with.

Because mastering the craft of software development requires constant practice and because the demand for good developers is always high, finding master craftsmen might seem impossible. Finding good people at short notice is hard in any field, so start looking early. Plenty of good, experienced developers are working on projects all over the place. Because they tend to stay with a project until it ships and goes live and then stay involved for future releases and enhancements, however, relatively few are ever looking for work—and they never have to look for long.

Use Your Old-timers

For most organizations, the best source of good, experienced developers is the pool of developers who have been working in the organization for a long time. Although the software engineering mindset would probably dismiss these people as old-timers who do not understand modern software engineering practices, this bad idea is a self-fulfilling prophesy. By valuing the developers who have been around for a long time and who really understand the current systems, we give them a real incentive to master their craft.

Valuing experienced developers enables organizations to view applications in a different light. Organizations can begin treating *software as capital*[65] and can provide investment funding to pay for

---

65. Baetjer, *Software as Capital.*

the continual update and upgrade of existing systems. Applications can then slowly evolve, rather than having organizations throw them away every five or so years and go through traumatic changes as new applications are created and installed. One of the basic tenets of software craftsmanship is that good developers with good tools can keep applications functional and maintainable practically indefinitely. Of course, they cannot do so if the underlying technology is changing rapidly or is declared obsolete by the vendor, so software craftsmanship values long-lived technologies and programming languages.

Mastery Implies the Use of Stable Technologies

Although software craftsmanship implies mastery of the software development tools, it is hard to justify the effort of learning a tool if it changes every six months and will be on the market for only five years. For example, experienced developers often questioned the claimed benefits of "new and improved" technologies such as 4GLs and RAD tools. In the end, these technologies just didn't have staying power. Even if a RAD tool is still available, it's almost impossible to take a five-year-old application and rebuild it in the latest version of a RAD tool.

Although 4GLs and RAD tools might be useful for building proof-of-concept prototypes, software craftsmen cannot use them for long-lived applications. Software craftsmen need programming environments that will last at least as long as the planned life of the application; few meet this criterion. Very few applications have a planned life of less than five years, whereas few software development tools are designed to be stable over that time frame.

Software Craftsmen Do Not Use Things Just Because They Are "the Latest and the Greatest"

Mastering the craft of software development brings with it the obligation to take a stand on important issues. This is a challenging part of software craftsmanship because it asks individuals to speak out and make their voices heard. The defining characteristic of master craftsmen is the ability to practice the craft without jumping on the latest bandwagon. This restraint is difficult to achieve in software development, because organizations are forever rolling out "new and improved" technologies with impressive fanfare and associated marketing hype. Unfortunately, most of these tools are targeted at the "dumbing down" of programming—something that software engineering has been advocating for years. Speaking out against the hype is not easy, but it is necessary when the hype is detrimental to the creation of robust, high-quality applications that can be used and extended for years.

Software craftsmanship offers an alternative to the "quick fix" technology solutions of software engineering. It questions the value of the plethora of new tools and programming languages and asks a simple question: "Why don't developers focus their attention on becoming really good at using the existing tools?" Some new tools may still be necessary, but any new tool must be measured against those already available, and the future evolution of the tool must be evaluated against the planned life of applications that will be built with it.

Software Engineering Has Been Trying to Kill COBOL for Decades

From the software craftsmanship standpoint, COBOL is a very effective and useful programming language. It has been available for more than 40 years and has a good track record for gradual evolution that does not break existing code. Even though countless businesses depend on mission-critical COBOL systems, the software engineering view states that COBOL is a dead language with no future. This view is expressed so strongly that organizations are now having to move away from COBOL because they cannot find developers who are willing to use it or courses to train new developers in this language.

The arguments supporting this position are somewhat strange. One organization explained that the reason it was moving away from COBOL and adopting Java was that it was impossible to find COBOL programmers. They couldn't find Java programmers either, so it planned a massive exercise to retrain everyone in Java. Crazy. It would have been much cheaper to set up training in COBOL for new hires rather than retrain the entire organization.

A lot of useful experience and wisdom about software development has been gained over the years by COBOL programmers, but it is not being tapped into because COBOL has been labeled a "legacy" language. Luckily, mastering software craftsmanship takes a long time, so most good, experienced developers have worked at one time or another in COBOL or in a similar vintage language. This past history gives them a special vantage point from which to view the hype with which new tools are promoted, allowing them to compare the new offerings against planned application lifetimes of 15 years or more. When looked at with an eye to the long view, it is no wonder that experienced developers prefer well-established technologies. Learning a new language or tool is not an issue for good developers. Most, however, have been burned at one time or another when a vendor ceased offering a tool. Experienced developers are wary of proprietary technologies, because they might not be available down the road when they are needed.

Developing Mastery Takes Time

Mastering software development is a slow process because developers need to create and then extend and enhance the application over several releases over a period of years. The process takes time because developers must learn to consider the effects of their decisions over the complete lifetime of a software application. It cannot be rushed, because software development requires that we pay attention to details. Indeed, it is only by living with and working on an application for years that a developer really learns what works and what does not work. By the time a developer has completed this process three or four times, he or she will be well on the way to mastering the craft of creating robust, high-quality, maintainable applications.

Achieving mastery of the craft of software development takes at least 15 years—probably longer. Of course, one can cite many examples of very young, talented programmers who have created fantastic programs, but software craftsmanship entails much more than solo programming. Talent is not the same as mastery. Mastery is the ability to create and successfully enhance robust, high-quality applications. It involves taking on the responsibility for maintaining an application for users and nurturing other developers so that when the time comes to move on to other applications, they will be ready and able to step into the maintainer's role.

Becoming a master software craftsman is not as simple as getting a certificate or passing an exam. Mastery is achieved by building a string of successful, robust, high-quality applications that lead to recognition by users, customers, and other developers. Developers know that they have achieved mastery of software craftsmanship when other developers seek them out to work with them, customers and managers want them to create applications, and users recommend their work. Building this kind of reputation takes time, but that is OK, because the applications that software craftsmen build are enduring as well.

Mastery Implies Taking Responsibility for Passing on the Craft

A key task for all master software craftsmen is taking apprentices and journeymen under their wing and providing an environment in which they can practice their craft. When master craftsmen undertake a project, either individually or with a few other master craftsmen, each craftsman will have one or two journeymen and apprentices working with them. A large project would then have 15 developers working on it: 3 craftsmen, 6 journeymen, and 6 apprentices. A small project would have only 3 developers: a craftsman, a journeyman, and an apprentice. A craftsman would never work on a project alone because of the overriding need to be able to pass the application on to a worthy successor when the time comes.

Craftsmen Choose Their Apprentices and Journeymen

Craftsmen have an incentive to provide good coaching and supervision to the people they take on because their reputations depend on the quality of the applications they produce. The change from software engineering practice, however, is that developers are not assigned to the craftsman. Rather, the craftsman chooses who will be their apprentice or journeyman, because the relationship is expected to last for a long time. It is not a case of a group of people getting together for a single project and then disbanding, but rather a team working together under a craftsman that takes on a series of projects. As such, accepting an apprentice is a long-term commitment for a master craftsman, and in undertaking this commitment, a developer acknowledges that she has become a master.[66]

---

66. When reviewing the book, Ken Auer pointed out: "You haven't really mastered something until you've taught it." In the process of explaining the concepts and providing coaching, you have to reflect on what you do, so you learn and improve your own mastery.

Chapter 12

Apprentice Developers

In the craft tradition, apprenticeship took a long time. Software craftsmanship is no different. The reason for this is that the quick "sheep dip" schooling model doesn't work well for a craft. Learning a craft entails lots of supervised and observed hands-on work, with the observation going both ways. The apprentice needs to see how the craftsman does a task just as much as a craftsman needs to oversee the work of the apprentice.

We can take the time needed to nurture apprentice developers because we are faced with the problem of abundance, rather than scarcity. We do not need hordes of software engineers, as software craftsmanship focuses on using small teams of good developers. Today we have more developers than needed, but we have a shortage of *good* developers. That is, we are in a Catch-22 situation: We don't have enough good developers, so we must find lots of warm bodies we can train. Because we need to train so many people, however, we cannot afford to train them properly.

We Must Reverse the Decline in the Quality of Developer Training

In the 1970s and early 1980s, training new developers was substantial and focused. A 13-week course in COBOL was not uncommon, with many induction programs running as long as 20 or 26 weeks. Even these longer courses covered only one or possibly two programming languages. After completing these courses, a trainee programmer would be assigned to work on a project under the supervision of an experienced programmer. Promotion to junior programmer would take between 6 and 18 months, during which time the trainee learned the basics of software development. It is no surprise, therefore, that many programmers nurtured in that environment have gone on to become great developers.

In the late 1980s and early 1990s, training courses were shortened drastically. Today, some courses pretend to teach Java programming in one week. Companies have stopped hiring trainees and now hire "experienced" developers, even if "experienced" means that the developer has used Java for 6 months. Some training organizations still provide 10- to 20-week courses for beginners, but these courses are paid for by the trainees and cover a wide range of programming languages. This change occurred because trainees have to cover all bases, as they never know which skills a hiring organization may need. The end result is that a trainee is given a 50- to 100-hour-long "sheep dip" in a disconnected variety of programming languages (typically 4–8).

Some of the better training organizations follow up these courses with an internship in a real project at an organization. Unfortunately, the supervision that the trainee receives in this circumstance from an experienced developer is generally nowhere nearly as good as it used to be. In fact, the trainee normally faces more of a "sink or swim" situation. A few trainees are lucky and manage to pick up effective software development habits, but many never really manage to progress beyond being perpetual novices.

Eventually, the trainee will end up on a project that uses one of the programming languages taught in the course, but that means that only 25% of the "training" was relevant. The other three to seven programming languages are soon forgotten because the trainee was never introduced to the craft of programming. Instead, he or she was taught only how to write code in various programming languages.

University Degrees Prepare Students for Academic Life, Not Real Projects

Few university courses prepare developers for working on real projects. The problem is that the schooling model employed by universities does not allow for enough coaching and mentoring. Rather than supporting collaborative development and reuse, these institutions typically view collaboration as cheating. In addition, university courses emphasize the rigorous, technical aspects of software development and in doing so, fail to cover the important "soft" skills that are part of becoming a great software developer. Courses cover compiler construction but fail to discuss requirements elicitation techniques or collaborative design. Overall, university courses provide a great theoretical background, but new graduates still have to learn the craft of software development.

Learning Software Development Is Not the Same as Being Taught How to Program

Learning a programming language is not hard, but it is incredibly difficult to learn a programming language taught by a teacher in a class. As Ted Nelson, an early computer visionary, said in 1974:

> *The best way to start programming is to have a terminal running an interactive language and a friend sitting nearby who already knows the language and has something else to do but can be interrupted with questions. And you just try stuff, till more and more you get the feel of it. And you find yourself writing programs that work.*[67]

That statement is just as true today as it was in 1974. Of the 16 or so programming languages I've used over the past 17 years, I'm much better at the ones I picked up without bothering to attend a training course.

The problem with attending a programming class is that teachers teach programming languages out of context. This approach is deadly, because most such classes are set up to prevent people from asking questions. Students learn at a very early stage that asking a question is pointless because the teacher does not have time to answer it. During a lesson on writing loops, for example, if a student asks a deep question about conditional logic, a typical answer might be, "We will cover that in the next lesson" or "We have already covered that." Neither response helps the student learn the programming language, and both reinforce the lesson that students should not ask questions.

---

67. Nelson, Ted, *Computer Lib*, Microsoft Press, 1987.

At a deeper level, the lack of context in programming classes hinders the development of wisdom. The lesson on writing loops fails to enlighten students about the circumstances under which it is appropriate to use a loop. Students are never shown how loops are used in larger applications. I've never seen a programming class that studied a 10,000-line annotated application that shows what is possible with the programming language and the correct, idiomatic use of the language.

If You Have to Send Beginners to Training, Make Sure It Is a Good Training Program

Beginners need to learn about the craft of programming and the ways in which the various programming languages express different concepts. This lesson must not entail a dry, academic comparison, but rather it must occur in a very practical, hands-on way. For example, beginners might build the same small application in two different languages. By reducing the number of languages used to two, trainees can focus on gaining a real appreciation for those two languages. Later, if it becomes necessary to learn a different programming language, picking up the new syntax will be relatively easy. After all, *writing the code is the easy part of software development.*

Going back to the old way of learning only one or two programming languages does not mean that the courses should be any shorter. By taking 10-to-20-week courses, trainees can tackle larger projects and come to appreciate some of the complexities of software development. With training and guided practice in all of the activities involved in software development, they will, in turn, be better prepared to participate in real projects. Once they have a good grounding in the craft of software development, trainees will know what questions to ask when they become members of project teams.

Apprenticeship Is More Effective Than Training to Learn a Craft

Whether a beginner starts out with a training course or is self-taught, the first step on the path to software craftsmanship is finding a craftsman to apprentice himself to. This has always happened, even in software engineering. Trainees find someone to go to with their questions and puzzles. Software craftsmanship, however, acknowledges that this search is a very important and significant step that should not be undertaken lightly. I was lucky in that my career began at a site where a very experienced and informative systems manager took a keen interest in the programming skills of all beginners. Although the relationship was informal and unrecognized, through chatting and talking while jobs compiled, he gave me a real sense of what software development was about and provided guidance and assistance with problems I encountered. Even though I had attended a 20-week training program, it was only through these conversations that I began to understand the career I had chosen.

Becoming an Apprentice Is a Significant Step

Through apprenticeship, software craftsmanship formalizes a coaching and mentoring relationship between a beginner and a master craftsman. In doing so, it provides organizational support for apprenticeship. Software craftsmanship acknowledges that having an apprentice takes time away from a craftsman's productive day, so it is unwise for a master craftsman to take on more than two apprentices. This loss of productive time can be attested to by many software engineering-influenced companies, where the senior developer is so busy supervising ten junior developers that he must stay late into the night just to get anything productive done.

Craftsmen Control the Impact on Their Work Through Careful Selection of Apprentices

Master craftsmen deal with the problem of trainees who require too much supervision by taking on only self-reliant and coachable apprentices. Apprenticeship is not a student–teacher relationship. Rather, the apprentice works under the guidance of someone whom she respects and wishes to emulate. Craftsmen take on only eager apprentices who are willing to learn the craft of software development. Instead of teaching the apprentices, the craftsman offers the opportunity to participate in software development projects in a manner that allows apprentices to learn for themselves how to become software craftsmen.

Apprenticeship Is More About Learning Than About Teaching

The apprenticeship model provides apprentices and journeymen with role models of effective behavior. The situated learning in the workplace[68] ensures that what is learned is relevant to the work-place and that the learners are motivated because they have a task to complete. This activity is the legitimate peripheral participation part of the apprenticeship model. Apprentices are required to be productive members of the team, and they learn how to ask for help, from either other apprentices or journeymen. In the traditional craft model, apprentices rarely asked questions directly of the master craftsman, thus allowing the master to stay productive.

Apprenticeship Is Not Schooling

Apprenticeship deliberately avoids the "learned helplessness" of the schooling model. Apprentices are expected to be self-reliant and require minimal supervision. This approach is in marked contrast to school, where dependency on the teacher to provide motivation, direction, and all answers is the norm.[69] Apprentices participate in real, meaningful, and important work. In addition, they derive satisfaction from their part in the delivery of an application.

An apprentice enters a trade to become a master of the craft. The motivation to succeed and excel is intrinsic, and completing an apprenticeship takes as long as it takes. An apprentice becomes a journeyman when ready, as judged by the apprentice as well as the master craftsman. In effect, everyone graduates with good marks—it's just that some take longer to graduate than others. As the skill of a journeyman reflects on the master, the graduation from apprentice to journeyman is a significant event.

Apprenticeship Instills Lifelong Learning

A significant role for an apprentice involves the coaching and mentoring of fellow apprentices. From a software engineering standpoint, this is crazy because it increases variability and compounds errors. Nevertheless, it has been used successfully for centuries. The reason why it succeeds can best be explained by looking at what happens in the martial arts. Novices are taught by intermediates, who are a few belts ahead of them. As the mistakes that the

---

68. Wenger, *Communities of Practice.*

69. Gatto, John Taylor, *Dumbing Us Down,* New Society Publishers, 1992.

intermediates make are magnified in the novices they teach, the master simply observes the novices to know how to correct the intermediates. After intermediates have learned the move correctly, they can then correct the novices. In this way, the form is preserved without the master being run ragged trying to coach everyone.

A master craftsman uses the same technique. By inspecting everything that the journeymen and apprentices create, the craftsman can provide useful coaching and feedback with minimal effort. This detailed review by the craftsman is possible because the master has to review the work of only a few people, and even then by performing a secondary review. That is, before the craftsman reviews an apprentice's work, it will have already been reviewed by the other apprentices and journeymen and cleaned up based on that feedback. Although the software engineering paradigm might consider this type of secondary review to be a waste of time, it is an essential part of practicing any craft. *Practice without feedback just reinforces errors.*

Apprentices Learn by Reviewing the Work of the Master

The review process goes both ways. Apprentices are expected to review everything that is produced by the team—craftsman, journeymen, and apprentices alike. By constantly being exposed to good work, apprentices pick up hard-to-explain nuances and get a feel for the craft of software development. This step also provides informal training in the aspects of software development to which apprentices have not yet been exposed. By reading and asking intelligent questions, apprentices will be able to pick up most skills without being formally taught. A final benefit of the apprentice reviewing everything is that it forces the journeymen and craftsman actually to practice what they preach.

Making sure that everyone has read everything that has been produced by the team insulates the team against the loss of any individual. As knowledge about the application is distributed among the entire team, no single person is key—not even the master craftsman. Even if the craftsman were hit by the hypothetical truck, the journeymen on the team would be drastically slowed down but would still make progress. The team would survive better than the equivalent software engineering team, because one of the keys to high productivity is in-depth knowledge of the entire application. Rather than lose time while a new developer tries to figure out what the departed team member was working on, a craft team can continue to make progress.

The Role of Apprentices

Apprentices have crucial, dual roles in software craftsmanship: They are productive software developers as well as questioning, inquisitive learners. These dual roles reinforce each other in many ways. Learning is never undirected because each apprentice has assigned tasks within a project. Thus the learning is motivated by the need to deliver something useful. Project tasks are also seen in their overall context because the apprentice is encouraged to be inquisitive about the entire software development process. Rather than just seeing disconnected tasks, an apprentice comes to see the whole picture and where his current piece fits in. Apprentices are also a source of the drive to improve the craft of software development because they are encouraged to question the way things are being done.

Apprentices are an essential part of software craftsmanship because they bring an enthusiasm and drive for learning that infect everyone else. Their drive and enthusiasm are channeled by initially giving them limited tasks. Additional tasks are added only when the initial tasks are performed well with minimal supervision.

In traditional crafts, apprentices graduate to new tasks only when they have trained a successor to perform the original task correctly. This choice is not very appropriate in software development, because there are few menial, low-skill tasks. Tasks that can be automated will be automated by craft teams, because that is the path to higher productivity. Thus apprentices are assigned small, meaningful tasks rather than menial, mundane tasks.

Apprentices Start with Low-Risk Applications

Ideally, apprentices will start working in the maintenance and enhancement of in-house tools and applications. By initially restricting apprentices to working on tools for the development team, we eliminate the possible risks to customer applications while giving the apprentices a grounding in and appreciation of the tools of the trade. The added benefit of this approach is that it encourages the development of productivity tools for software development. Unlike the traditional software engineering approach, however, apprentices are closely supervised. They work closely with journeymen and master craftsmen, who carefully review everything they do. The apprentices must master the in-house development tools and applications before they can progress to enhancing and modifying these tools and applications.

Apprentices Progress to Working on Customer Applications

Once an apprentice has proved to be proficient in the team's development tools, she is ready to undertake small enhancement and maintenance tasks on customers' applications. Initially, these jobs would consist of well-specified coding or testing tasks to be worked on in conjunction with another apprentice or journeyman. As the apprentice's proficiency grows, she would take on larger, less well-specified tasks that include the design and analysis aspects of software development. Throughout this stage, the apprentice would be expected to sit in on all analysis and design meetings as well as review everything produced by the craft team. Thus, although the apprentice may not have actually specified the design at hand, she will have been present when it was created and discussed with the team. It will become obvious to the craftsmen and journeymen that an apprentice is ready to take on design duties when she begins making real contributions in the design sessions.

Progression for an Apprentice Occurs Through Demonstrated Competence

Progression in an apprenticeship is not a matter of passing exams. Progression occurs when apprentices are competent in the performance of their current tasks and have picked up enough about another related task to be able to perform it at a minimum level. This minimum level is set rather high compared with the levels established for software engineering trainees, because apprentices are expected to spend a portion of every day practicing and learning about the tasks related to the ones they already know.

Thus, although apprentices are expected to perform at a high level and produce competent work, apprenticeship is not about cheap labor. Apprentices are expected to do productive work because it is really the best way to learn software development. It is in everyone's interest for them to improve rapidly so that they need less supervision.

Apprentices Are Not Cheap Labor

Unlike software engineering, software craftsmanship takes a long-term view of things. Although it is possible to use apprentices as cheap labor, in the long run this is inefficient. If an apprentice is on average one-fifth as productive as the journeyman who is coaching him or her, then why load work on an apprentice to the point where the trainee has no time to learn? If, by giving an apprentice a lighter load and good coaching, we can bring him up to the level of a journeyman in four or five years, then in the last year alone the apprentice will do as much work as possible by assigning an initially heavy workload. Rather than getting 6 units of work out of two people, we can eventually get at least 15 units of work from the same people (because the experienced journeyman is no longer slowed down by the need to supervise the trainee closely).[70]

This analysis understates actually the benefit because, over the course of an apprenticeship, the journeyman will be learning and improving as well. Indeed, in many cases journeymen will learn from apprentices as the following story from Ken Auer shows:

> Michael, an apprentice, was working with Jeff, a journeyman at the studio. They were trying to figure out how to convert a desktop application into a JSP/Servlet-based Web application. Jeff shared how amazing it was when they worked together. Jeff has a family and other responsibilities at Role Model and couldn't devote the "extracurricular" time to reading all the articles written on learning about potential techniques of applying the technology that Michael could. Often, they would reach the end of a day stuck. In the morning, Michael would show Jeff a couple of articles he found and thought might have some potential, highlighting relevant sections. Jeff would then look them over and analyze them in ways that Michael could not. Then they would work together toward a new approach.[71]

An Apprenticeship Is a Significant Investment of Time and Energy

An apprenticeship will last at least five years. Although this period might seem like an eternity to people accustomed to "Internet time,"

---

70. Cockburn, Alistair, *Surviving Object Oriented Projects*, Addison-Wesley, 1998.

71. Ken Auer, Role Model Software, Inc., personal communication.

it is comparable to the time that it takes in many other fields to go from being a complete novice to being able to undertake sizable projects with minimal supervision.

The length of the apprenticeship could be shorter if the apprentice had a computing degree, but it would probably be more effective to become an apprentice before starting the degree. The apprentice would then receive academic teaching and would be working on real projects simultaneously, making the experience become a sort of co-op degree on steroids.

Apprenticeship takes a long time because it takes time to absorb the culture and ethics of a craft. A key problem with software development is that the knowledge of how to do something is ineffective without the wisdom that comes from deep understanding of the underlying reasons. Developing this deep understanding takes time. The lack of it explains why many projects are so stressed. That is, *we know how to develop great software*, but many developers still don't take the necessary steps. Software craftsmanship solves this problem by taking the time to instill the proper attitudes and values into apprentices before allowing them to move on to more independent work.

Apprentices Become Journeymen When They Are Ready for That Responsibility

The transition from apprentice to journeyman is very significant because it represents a public acknowledgment by a master craftsman that the apprentice is now capable of creating small applications without any assistance. No certification or licensing is involved. Rather, the craftsman puts his reputation on the line by stating that the individual has completed his apprenticeship and is now worthy of being called a journeyman.

Apprentices do not automatically become journeymen. That is, they do not serve their time and automatically get promoted. Becoming a journeyman depends on the ability of an apprentice to demonstrate her competence to the craftsmen she works with every day.

Chapter 13

Journeymen Developers

The step from apprentice to journeyman is very significant and represents the coming of age of the developer. It is a public recognition that the developer is a skilled generalist, able to undertake application development projects without assistance. Customers, managers, and other craftsmen will be able to verify this ability by looking at the last application on which the journeyman worked as an apprentice. This "graduation" application is the start of the portfolio that the journeyman will build from successfully created applications.

In becoming a journeyman, a developer accepts responsibility for creating robust, high-quality applications and confirms her acceptance of the software craftsmanship approach. In the traditional crafts, journeymen would often travel to work with other craftsmen to hone their skills while earning enough money to set up shop as an independent. In software development, the economic need to work for other craftsmen is less, but the need to broaden and hone skills is greater. Software craftsmen tend to specialize in just a few programming languages, so journeymen need to work with different craftsmen to broaden their experience until they find the languages in which they want to specialize. Similarly, for application domains, because customers like to use the same few trusted craftsmen repeatedly, to get experience with different customers a journeyman will have to work with different craftsmen.

Where Journeymen Fit in the Craft Tradition

In the craft tradition, two main paths were open to journeymen. The first path was to strive to produce a "masterpiece," something that was worthy of the journeyman being judged a master of the craft. Attaining this level of mastery of a craft requires transcending the skills and coming to identify oneself as a master craftsman, a peer of all other craftsmen. It is as much about attitude as it is about competence, even though competence is a prerequisite. On this path, being a journeyman is about practicing the craft to develop the technique and artistry needed to become a master craftsman. Once a journeyman's masterpiece was accepted as such by the fellow craftsmen, it was then exhibited as an advertisement to potential customers.

The second path for a journeyman was probably more common. Rather than striving for mastery, he could continue working for other craftsmen for his entire career. This path explains why the word "journeyman" is associated with a solid, hard-working approach that, although possibly lacking in artistry, is functional and gets the job done.

Journeymen Developers

Regardless of the path that a journeyman takes, he or she will be much more effective than an average developer in the software engineering tradition. How can I make this assertion? Simple. After working closely with a master craftsman for four or five years in an environment that encourages learning, it would be hard to be worse than the average programmer. Working in a closely knit team where everyone reviews one another's work on a daily basis means that, even without trying, a journeyman will gain a real breadth of experience about software development. Rather than forcing them into a narrow specialization early on, software craftsmanship insists that developers remain aware of and contribute to the entire process of application development, even if they want to specialize.

Journeymen Rarely Work Alone

Although a journeyman could undertake an application alone, unless it was small and unimportant, such a course of action would not be a good idea. As a minimum, a journeyman should always work with another journeyman or a craftsman so that knowledge of the details of the application is in at least two heads. If the journeyman works with a craftsman, then an apprentice would also be part of the team. After all, it is hard to be an apprentice to a craftsman when the craftsman is working on a different project.

Journeymen Are Focused on Delivering Applications

Always putting at least two people on an application may be a change for managers and customers, but one of the goals of software craftsmanship is application delivery. With three applications to be developed and three developers, all three developers can work together to deliver one application quickly and then move on to the next task. Giving an application to each developer is crazy. Sure, it looks like more is happening, and managers can tell a customer "We are working on your application," but it takes longer to deliver a working application.

Journeymen have an incentive to work in teams because that structure allows them to complete applications faster. Quick delivery is useful because it adds another application to the developer's portfolio. Shipping is important because it is when developers learn what it takes to develop great applications—users provide lots of feedback once an application is live. Maintaining and enhancing live applications give journeymen the best environment for improving their craft, as they are expected to respond to business requests in hours or days. With a short feedback cycle, it is very easy to learn what works and what does not work.

For the same reasons, journeymen prefer to work in small teams. There is little value in being part of a very large team, because their contributions are unlikely to stand out. Small teams make for efficient communication, and the collaboration between developers in a small team often makes for an even better application than any one of the developers could have created alone. Small teams are preferred, however, because having more than four people in a team makes communication harder and less efficient. Large teams also mean long-duration projects or short-term, very stressful projects, both of which are a sign that projects are being organized using software engineering principles. Software craftsmanship aims to create applications using small, highly skilled teams. If a customer needs an application built quickly, he or she should hire craftsmen rather than journeymen. Similarly, rather than building a single, large application with a really big team, the craft approach would ask whether it was possible to create several cooperating applications using small craft teams.

Journeymen Play a Key Role in Software Craftsmanship

Journeymen provide the bulk of the training and mentoring to apprentices on behalf of craftsmen. Although apprentices apprentice themselves to a craftsman, in reality an apprentice joins a small community of developers working under that craftsman. When accepting a journeyman from outside, a craftsman will look very carefully to ensure that she will fit in with the other journeymen and apprentices because like apprentices, each journeyman will work with a craftsman for a long time. What is important is the long-term success of the relationship, not the immediate need to fill a vacancy.

A key difference between software craftsmanship and software engineering is the emphasis that craftsmanship puts on learning and coaching. Craftsmanship recognizes that, in the end, software development is constrained by communication between people and the ability of small teams to learn rapidly and effectively. As such, it selects people who are willing to learn and then gives them lots of opportunities to practice coaching each other. This provides the foundation on which to build really effective small teams of journeymen led by a craftsman. These small teams then provide an ideal environment in which to nurture apprentices so that they can mature into journeymen.

PART 4

Repositioning Software Engineering

Software craftsmanship is not a replacement for software engineering, but rather a complement to it. Software engineering emerged to solve the problem of creating really large, multiple-year systems development projects such as air traffic control systems. Software craftsmanship is an acknowledgment that, for smaller applications, all we have ever needed was to give the application to a few good developers. Scaling down software engineering to deal with smaller problems is just as hard as scaling up the craftsmanship approach—and just as inappropriate.

Repositioning software engineering is necessary because one of the classical problems in software engineering has been *getting engineers to use effective methods consistently.*[72] What software engineering means by *effective methods* does not always equate to effective behavior in a smaller team. For small teams, craftsmanship is more appropriate because we can trust individuals to do what it takes to create and maintain applications. As the *Borland Software Craftsmanship* study showed, small teams of good developers can produce

---

72. Humphrey, Watts, in *Why Don't They Practice What We Preach?* http://www.sei.cmu.edu/publications/articles/practice-preach/practice-preach.html.

great applications. The upper bound for craftsmanship is probably reached with between 10 and 15 developers. Also, although a craft team would normally stay together for years, releases would occur frequently—normally spaced no more than months apart.

Some problems, however, cannot be solved by a small team of good developers. Some problems truly require a large team to deal with all of their complexities and interdependencies, and it is these problems that are within the domain of software engineering. Repositioning software engineering means that we define a threshold above which the software engineering approach becomes appropriate. A reasonable threshold would be projects larger than 100 developer-years, say, requiring more than 50 developers for more than two years.

For projects smaller than 100 developer-years, a software craftsmanship approach is more effective. As shown by the *Borland Software Craftsmanship* study, a small team of great developers can readily deliver applications that would require the services of a much larger team using a software engineering approach.

So, with these definitions in place, it is time to shift our focus and see what repositioned software engineering projects would look like. We will also look at lessons learned from software engineering that can be usefully incorporated into software craftsmanship.

Chapter 14

Software Engineering Projects

Software engineering is not the same as software craftsmanship because the former attempts to solve a different problem. Craftsmanship is a solution to the problem of delivering robust, high-quality applications to users in a relatively short time for reasonable cost. Software engineering is a solution to a different set of problems, involving life- or safety-critical systems, real-time and embedded systems, and systems engineering projects. In these types of problems, fast delivery and reasonable cost are not the driving factors on the project, so a craftsmanship approach is not the best one. Software engineering projects typically involve both hardware and software, often stretching the envelope on one or the other dimension.

The driving factors on software engineering projects usually consist of a combination of functionality, performance, and verification. As such, the problem is not one of simply creating the software and then passing some acceptance tests. Rather, verification and validation are major challenges. Software engineering projects often take many years, because unlike most applications they are designed either to run on special hardware or to operate special hardware. In either case, the special hardware is often not available when the project starts, because it is being designed or invented as part of the overall project.

Software engineering, therefore, has to deal with the problem of developing software where incremental development and evolutionary delivery are not feasible strategies. Examples would be avionics for a new airplane, software for a next-generation cell phone, and pacemakers and other medical electronics. In all of these cases, a project could easily be halfway over before even prototype hardware becomes available. In many cases, the final hardware version remains in flux until very late in the project. As soon as it is finalized and released to manufacturing, the pressure is on to certify that everything works correctly.

Software Engineering Is Designed for Large Systems Projects

With these sorts of engineering project constraints, it was natural that the *software engineering* metaphor was created, because engineering the software was just a small part of the overall project. Not surprisingly, practices that worked well in mechanical and aero-related engineering were tried and applied to software development. Specifications were documented in exquisite detail, validated, verified, and signed off. Designs were worked on, reviewed, documented, and subjected to verification, and validation with all items traced back to the original specifications. Engineering change orders, just like those found in the hardware world, had to go through multiple levels of review to determine the total impact that they would have on everyone else. When the target hardware became available, the designs could then be handed over to the coding team for the minor detail of programming and implementation.

This approach to software engineering is natural when the target hardware does not become available until near the end of the project. There is no point in coding early, because there is no hardware on which to run the code. Hence analysis, design, and verification are very important, because they are the predominant activities for most of the project. After spending so much time on the design work, programming is just the mere matter of coding, but that coding must be subjected to substantial verification and validation to ensure that it matches the design.

Specialization Is Natural for Software Engineers

It is natural for engineers to have specialities in software engineering projects because the activities are spaced out over time. It is also natural for engineers to talk about a requirements phase, a design phase, a coding phase, and a test phase because each activity occurs sequentially and dominates all others for months at a time. During the requirements (or analysis) phase, other activities may be taking place (such as design sketches, simulations, or experiments), but all of the work is focused on understanding the problem and the constraints that exist on possible solutions. During the design phase, even if some requirements clarification is still occurring, the focus is on creating and verifying a really detailed design that satisfies all of the requirements and can be implemented. Yes, some programming experiments may take place, but they are intended to test the validity of design ideas, rather than to start "production coding" early.

Software Engineering Projects Still Use the Waterfall Process

Although the software engineering world pays "lip service" to the idea that the "waterfall" software development life cycle is ineffective, it remains the predominant process. Even the job descriptions that are used tie into the phases in the waterfall: analyst, designer, programmer, and tester. Incremental development is sometimes used, but that typically mean incremental programming and testing once the analysis and design phases are complete.

Programming Should Be a Mechanical Activity in Software Engineering Projects

Once a detailed design specification has been produced and validated, the last thing that software engineering projects need is programmers who get creative and try to improve the design. Ideally, the engineering will employ tools that can automatically generate the required code from the detailed designs or, failing that, programmers who will just write code according to the specification. To ensure that this is happening, some projects have detailed "code walkthroughs" where a group will carefully go through a short section of code, line by line, looking for mistakes and potential problems. Some groups will even do so before attempting to compile the code because knowing that the code compiles means that the reviewers are less likely to catch some kinds of errors. Careful statistics are kept about these reviews. Reviews that find an unusual number of mistakes (above or below the expected numbers) signal that something is different about the process. In effect, software engineering tries to bring the coding activities under what manufacturing calls *statistical process control.*

Software Development Is Not the Rate Limiting Step in Software Engineering Projects

Software engineering practices are predicated on the fact that *developing the software is not the rate-limiting step in the overall project.* Although the software needs a lot of people and takes a lot of time, compared with the overall project timeline, developing the software is not what determines the overall project completion date. Yes, there are counterexamples of projects being held up because of late software, but this is natural because software development activities dominate at the end of a project. Hence any delays in earlier parts of a project show up at the end and are often attributed to software development, even though the actual slippage was caused by a different upstream activity.

Software engineering differs from application development because of its different time pressures. In application development, software development is the rate-limiting step. If the software can be developed faster, the application can be released earlier. Conversely, in software engineering projects, developing the software sooner doesn't help if the hardware is still changing rapidly. This crucial distinction explains the difference between software engineering and software craftsmanship. Craftsmanship is focused on delivering applications on known hardware to known users, whereas software engineering represents only a small part of a much larger project to deliver a hardware/software combination to a customer.

Software Engineering Projects Are Diverse and Varied

It is hard to provide a simple characterization of software engineering projects because of the range of project sizes that must be addressed—from small, 100-person-year projects to extremely large, 10,000-person-year projects (and beyond). Small software engineering projects generally tend to be more productive and less risky, than extremely large projects, but to some extent that can be explained by the difficulty in communicating among large groups of people. There is also the problem of finding enough developers to staff these large projects, because few developers have any experience working on really large software engineering projects. Instead, such projects are staffed with lots of junior developers, leading to the accusation that software engineering focuses on how to run projects with hordes of average developers.

This characterization is unfair. Some large software development projects use a software engineering approach because they are stretching the envelope in terms of size. For these projects, it is not always possible to find enough great developers. The software engineering approach allows an organization to use average developers because the process compensates for their lack of experience. The various reviews and controls on the project deliverables enable average teams to do a good job at delivering large applications.

Agile Methodologies Are an Alternative to Systematic Software Engineering Processes

Although many software development methodologies have been heavily influenced by software engineering, a few are driven by the ways that people work and learn. A recently formed Agile Alliance[73] has attempted to make the case for the importance of individuals over process. The Agile Alliance was formed by a group of developers and methodologists to counter the perceived wisdom that the only correct way to do software development is through a process- and document-driven software engineering approach.

The Agile Alliance offers a strong alternative to the traditional software engineering way of doing software development. By rejecting the process-driven approach, the Agile Methodologies focus attention on the individuals in the software development team and the quality of their interactions with their customers and users. In doing so, they provide a good fit with software craftsmanship and another voice warning about the hazards of the software engineering approach.

---

73. http://www.agilealliance.org/.

Chapter 15

Hazards of the Software Engineering Metaphor

Although software engineering is an excellent approach for some projects, it is an inappropriate choice for most commercial software development. Software engineering is not optimized to provide what commercial projects need—namely, rapid delivery of robust, high-quality applications at reasonable cost. Unfortunately, because the software engineering metaphor is so powerful, many attempts have been made to force-fit this approach to other types of software development. This has proved to be very hazardous for some projects.

You Cannot Do Software Engineering on a Low Budget

As the experience with the space shuttle software showed, the software engineering approach can produce near-perfect software but is very expensive. That expense is a natural consequence of the many detail reviews, inspections, and cross-checks that occur between all of the deliverables in software engineering projects. If you attempt to speed up the process drastically or cut back on costs, you have stopped doing software engineering. You might still call the process by that name, but you are not very likely to produce near-perfect software by following that path.

Faster, Better, Cheaper or on Time, on Budget, on Mars—Pick Two

In recent years, NASA has been experimenting with a *faster, better, cheaper* approach. It works—NASA gets things done on time and on budget. The cost, however, is a much higher risk of failure.[74] The *Mars Polar Lander*, for example, failed because of software errors.[75] Cheap software engineering is not software engineering. Going low budget is just that—a risky shortcut to producing dubious software. To get a faster, cheaper, better solution, you need to use a different approach.

Believe the Estimates—Software Engineering Projects Take a Lot of Time

Much anecdotal evidence suggests that projects are late and exceed their budget. These stories are probably true. Many projects do exceed the time they are planned to take.[76] I see much less evidence, however, that they exceed the time that they were *estimated to take*. The problem is one of *gutless estimating*, not of delayed projects. To put it more politely, these projects suffer from *excessive schedule pressure*.

This excessive schedule pressure is a hazard of the software engineering metaphor. In the mechanical world, if something is taking too long, you can simply make the people work harder and longer. This tactic works every time. After all, everyone knows that workers are lazy and will slack off whenever they get the opportunity.[77] The best way to apply pressure is to give the workers a stretch target. This idea is utter stupidity when it comes to software development.

---

74. *NASA FBC Task Final Report*, www.hq.nasa.gov/pub/pao/reports/2000/ fbctask.pdf.

75. *Report of the Mars Program Independent Assessment Team*, http:// www.nasa.gov/newsinfo/marsreports.html.

76. Glass, Robert L., *Software Runaways*, Prentice-Hall, 1998.

77. Taylor, F. W., *The Principles of Scientific Management*, 1911 (online at http:// www.therblig.com/taylor/title.html).

Software Engineering Encourages Scientific Management

In the old-style factories of the Industrial Revolution, people were hired to work, not to think. There was a process to follow, and you did what you were told. As much as possible, the machines embodied the knowledge, and the people were trained to operate the machines. The ultimate expression of this concept was the production line, where the workers were trained in one very specialized, simple task. Although in a strictly monetary economic sense the production line worked, its dehumanizing effects were satirized as early as the era of silent films by Charlie Chaplin.

The ideas of scientific management were very effective at optimizing manual work. Frederick W. Taylor enumerated the principles of scientific management as a way to get more productivity from unskilled, manual labor:

> *First. They develop a science for each element of a man's work, which replaces the old rule of thumb method.*
>
> *Second. They scientifically select and then train, teach, and develop the workman, whereas in the past he chose his own work and trained himself as best he could.*
>
> *Third. They heartily cooperate with the men so as to insure all of the work being done in accordance with the principles of the science which has been developed.*
>
> *Fourth. There is an almost equal division of the work and the responsibility between the management and the workmen. The management take over all work for which they are better fitted than the workmen, while in the past almost all of the work and the greater part of the responsibility were thrown upon the men.*[78]

These ideas were so successful at improving the output of unskilled labor that they took hold of the industrialized world in the 1920s and 1930s. They have continued to dominate management thinking through to the present day. In fact, the ideas are so pervasive that we rarely stop even to think about them. The very success of scientific management makes it practically impossible to imagine

---

78. Taylor, *The Principles of Scientific Management.*

alternatives, and it completely dominates the conversation because it defined the vocabulary.

Software Engineering Denigrates Anecdotal Evidence

Scientific management substituted science for the rule of thumb. In this approach, numbers rule. To improve something, first you have to measure it. If something cannot be measured, it is unimportant. Management knows best. There is one best way to do any job.

In the mechanical world, this concept truly works. Through the use of "scientific shoveling," the Bethlehem Steel Works got laborers to move nearly four times as much pig iron in one day for only 60% higher wages—a fantastic win all around. The workers were paid more, and output rose enough to enable the management to pay the workers more.

Small wonder, then, that software engineering has invented lots and lots of ways to measure software development. The time-and-motion studies that came out of scientific management have even been applied to studying the usability of software. Quantitative laws have been identified concerning issues such as how long it takes to move a cursor over a button (Fitts's law[79]) and how long it takes to choose between equally probable courses of action (Hick's law).

In the mania for measurement, people sometimes forget to distinguish between mechanical actions and mental actions. Fitts's law primarily concerns a mechanical action, although it is complicated by the need for eye–hand coordination, Hick's law attempts to measure what is going on in a person's head. Here software engineering is making a classical mistake: It is assumes that what it can measure is important. It is not.

Software development is predominantly a mental activity. Typing never has been, and never will be, the rate-limiting step in software development. The only way to talk about such mental activities is through anecdotes, because the measurements you can make are irrelevant for improving performance. Software engineering is hazardous because it downplays the value of the only mechanism we have for really understanding and improving software development—anecdotes that developers tell one another.

---

79. Raskin, Jef, *The Humane Interface*, Addison-Wesley, 2000.

Software Factories: The Production Line for Software

Software factories are a natural extension of the idea of scientific management. After all, production lines are really effective; they will be great for software development. With a software factory we can benefit from standardized processes and reusable components. This idea is a great concept, but again it confuses mechanical and mental activities.

A standard process that can be used across multiple projects is certainly appealing. This commonality would make it easier to deploy staff across different projects and would lead to greater efficiencies. In practice, this process works only if the teams and projects are practically identical. Also, the realities of the software market are such that it is often preferable to buy an existing package than to wait for a customized solution. Instead of seeking out a software factory to get a customized accounting package, then, customers choose from one of the many competing packaged solutions.

Cross-Project Reuse Is Very Hard to Achieve

It is hard to make internally developed components reusable. Internal reuse within a project is achievable, but reuse across projects is very difficult. Indeed, Alistair Cockburn suggests that we should really call it PolyBloodyHardReuse[80] because a simple word like "reuse" implies that this task is easy. Truly reusable components are possible, but these are not internally developed components. Reusable components need an entire organization dedicated to their creation and support. The issue here is use, not reuse. Oracle, for example, sells a popular database used by many companies. Development tools ship with large class libraries of handy components that are more or less ready to use.

Software factories represent an attempt to emulate the manufacturing world as it used to be. Manufacturing, however, has moved on. Even the most avid production-line fan no longer talks about

---

80. Cockburn, *Surviving Object Oriented Projects*.

completely integrated manufacture. Car companies no longer own steel mills, coal mines, and rubber plantations. Instead, they buy their tires from organizations that are good at making tires. The same is true for software components. By using readily available components, even small teams can produce great software.

The concept of a software factory has not really caught on because manufacturing software is easy. The difficulty lies in creating and evolving the design for the software in collaboration with the users of that software.

Reuse over Time Is Hazardous

One advantage attributed to software factories was that over time they theoretically would build up a repository of reusable software that would enable them to become highly efficient. While this idea is seductive from a mechanical viewpoint, it fails to recognize the unique characteristics of the software environment. As Gordon Moore, the co-founder of Intel, pointed out in 1964, computers double in power every 18 months. The implications of this statement are rarely noticed by the proponents of reuse.

Software is written to the limitations of current hardware. We had the Y2K fiasco because in the 1970s it made sense to save the cost of the extra memory required for the two century digits. As the same software was used over and over again the original reason for dropping the century digits no longer applied. Similarly, the European Space Agency's *Arianne 5* failure was caused by the reuse of software from the successful *Arianne 4* launcher:

> *The internal SRI software exception was caused during execution of a data conversion from 64-bit floating point to 16-bit signed integer value. The floating point number, which was converted, had a value greater than what could be represented by a 16-bit signed integer. This resulted in an Operand Error.*[81]

A 16-bit signed integer is a holdover from the very early days of computing. It is a compact way of storing small numbers (smaller

---

81. *Ariane 5 Flight 501 Failure Report by the Inquiry Board*, www.esa.int/htdocs/tidc/Press/Press96/ariane5rep.html.

than 32,768) that requires only 2 bytes of memory. Software once used 16-bit integers widely because of their efficiency. Old 16-bit software continues to be reused to this day. Unfortunately, as the failure of *Arianne 5*, which had a different launch trajectory than *Arianne 4*, proved, not all numbers can be represented by 16 bits.

The problem was that old demon—the mechanical metaphor. As the inquiry report said, "The view had been taken that *software should be considered correct until it is shown to be at fault* [emphasis added]." While this view might work for mechanical things, it fails miserably for software. Software is weird stuff. Reuse is safe only after careful consideration and investigation. Reuse over time is particularly hazardous because knowing that the software worked well in the past means that we are not suspicious enough. Have you ever wondered why your word processor scrolls the text much too fast when you are selecting text? You have been hit by the hazard of reuse over time. Modern machines are so much faster that instead of selecting a few lines, you have just selected ten pages.

The Myth of the Standardized Software Development Process

The software engineering metaphor makes us believe that software development is manual labor. It makes us believe that the *division of labor* is a good thing that should be used in software development. It makes us believe that there are standard *best practices* that everyone should adopt. This notion is not true, however. Software development is different. As Jim Highsmith has pointed out, *having a process is not the same as having the skills to carry out that process.*[82] This idea explains why software factories don't work nearly as well as real factories. In a real factory, the process can be broken down into finely detailed steps, so that the mechanical skills to perform the process can be easily learned in a few hours or days. Hence, most factory workers are classified as unskilled labor because their training does not take very long.

---

82. Highsmith, *Adaptive Software Development*.

In contrast, the steps in a software development process are very large, and significant skills are required to perform the process. It is impossible to run a software development process with unskilled labor. Although plenty of projects have tried, none has succeeded. Software development occurs in the heads of the developers and is expressed in documentation, drawings, and source code. The more finely a task is broken down into small steps, the more time is spent passing information from one person to another.

Instead of thinking of software engineering as manual labor in a factory, it would be better to think of it as the process whereby a factory and associated production line are designed and built. Unfortunately, few people have any real knowledge of what it takes to build a production line, so the metaphor they choose is the more familiar one of working on the production line.

The Traditional Division of Labor Does Not Work for Software Development

The division of labor causes multiple hand-offs among analyst, designer, programmer, tester, user interface specialist, technical writer, and support staff. Projects take forever, changes cause chaos as the new information gets passed down the development chain, and software becomes "legacy applications" because nobody really understands how it all works.

By creating artificial specialties with narrow skill sets, software engineering makes it impossible for one person to understand the entire application. Rather than encouraging developers to cross-train so that they can understand all of an application, software engineering promotes the myth that what is needed instead is good documentation. Unfortunately, although documentation is very good for recording decisions and agreements, it is a very ineffective way of preserving and communicating detailed knowledge of how a software application actually works. Software engineering has given documentation a very bad name. Many projects practically run without any documentation because inexperienced developers rebel against this software engineering view.

Best Practices Are a Holdover from the One Best Way of Scientific Management

The very term "best practices" is a holdover from scientific management. How can you be against using a best practice? Easy. Best practices work well in the mechanical world, but they do not apply to mental activities.

Never forget that it is people who imagine, design, and develop software. Although some mechanical best practices are applicable (making backups of everything or testing on the complete range of target hardware), none addresses the most important parts of software development—imagination and design. Best practices are a hazard because they ask us to substitute slogans for thinking.

Best Practices Reinforce the Lesson That It Is Not OK to Fail Differently

The faster, better, cheaper review at NASA showed that although it is OK to *succeed* differently, it can be a career-limiting move to *fail* differently. Indeed, if you fail in anything other than the approved, best-practice manner, the successes you did have will be ignored. At times it seems that best practices exist just to keep the workers in their place, following orders.

Best Practices Actively Hinder Process Innovation

Organizations tend to adopt a process more for the purposes of oversight and control than with a view to improving the effectiveness of delivery. They attempt a "one size fits all" approach because it is easier to treat all projects in the same way. The strange result is that teams end up working off-process just to make progress, though they normally pretend they are following the process.

Sometimes these off-process projects accidentally stumble on a combination of software development practices that allows them to be spectacularly successful compared with projects following the standardized process. The software developers deliver the system to a satisfied user community and are fired up and enthusiastic about spreading the word about how good their process is. If they are enthusiastic enough and create an appropriately catchy name, the new process many be adopted by the rest of the company or outside of the company in different projects. Converts to this new process then become enthusiastic and push to have this new process adopted as the "one size fits all" standard.

The originators of the new process are then placed in an awkward position. They understand that they were successful because of the special circumstances of their project that allowed their new process to be successful, yet their converts make claims about the new process, claims that are not backed up by project experience. In many cases, the unfortunate consequence is that the hype wins and the new process is adopted in projects for which it is not suitable. The game is then set up for a whole new round of innovators to create another new process variant, allowing the cycle to continue.

Software Engineering Forces Us to Forget the Individual

As Alistair Cockburn pointed out in *Characterizing People as Nonlinear, First-Order Components in Software Development*,[83] software engineering fails to pay attention to the most important component of the software development process—the people. The most likely reason for this omission is that individuals show up only in small teams. The early work of Gerald Weinberg and Tom deMarco, which looked at the role of the individual, emerged from smaller projects. In fact, much of their work could be described as telling stories about what really happens in smaller teams.

One result of ignoring the people in the team is that most software development processes that are defined deal with large team issues. We get a macro-process definition that deals with the big picture, but rarely do we get a detailed micro-process definition that states what the individuals on a team are supposed to do. Although the better processes do describe the various roles needed in the development process, rarely do they talk about how those roles will be distributed among the various members of a small team.

Software Developers Are Not Interchangeable Resources

Software engineering makes us think of developers as human resources. As a result, we may forget that developers will actually learn as the project progresses. For this reason, many job advertisements tend to overspecify the required skill sets: "Must have at least two years Java 1.3 and Swing experience creating CRM applications on Windows 2000." Aside from making us think that a skills shortage exists, these ads make the mistake of assuming that developers are interchangeable. They are not. Technical knowledge

---

83. http://members.aol.com/humansandt/papers/nonlinear/nonlinear.htm.

is much less important than the ability to integrate well with the rest of the development team.

Thus, forgetting that developers can learn and just thinking of them as interchangeable resources, software engineering creates an artificial skills shortage. This result is a natural outcome of software engineering—forgetting the individual.

Software engineering is hazardous because software development is not egalitarian. Good developers make the difference between project success and failure. Good developers can always pick up a new technology. I'm not interested in hiring a six-pack of certified Java developers, but I am interested in finding good people who can contribute to an existing team. For all but the shortest of projects, there will be time for developers to learn and experiment with the bits of technology that they do not initially know.

Faking a Rational Development Process

In 1986, Parnas and Clements wrote a paper titled "A Rational Process: How and Why to Fake It"[84] to address the issue of developers who needed to show a logical derivation of a completed deliverable. The suggestion was that we document systems to show that this design element arose from an analysis decision based on that requirement. Doing so allows readers of the document to see the overall logical structure, even though the project was not actually done in that way. Readers are not interested in the detours taken along the way, just in what the final version looks like and the reasons it looks that way.

Unfortunately, when this document is seen through software engineering-tinted glasses that hide the people, *we are left with the impression that we should be able to capture all of the requirements first*, then do the design, then code, and then test. Luckily for the users of software, most developers ignore this approach because they realize that requirements emerge as the users see the evolving design. Later they may have to apologize for not following the process or (as Parnas and Clements suggest) fix up the paper trail to make it look like they followed a rational process. So, rather than employing a systematic approach that helps developers, software

---

84. Parnas, D. L., and Clements, P. C., "A Rational Design Process: How and Why to Fake It," *IEEE Transactions on Software Engineering*, February 1986.

engineering often causes developers to apologize for starting design work before all of the requirements were known, even if that is the only way they can actually deliver a useful system.

We Need More Variety in Our Development Processes, Not Less

The software development community as a whole does not understand how to talk about software development. We do not seem to be able to explain why software development is so variable and unpredictable. We need to find a way to explain that. When it comes to ways of developing software, one size definitely does not fit everyone. Therefore we need to find a way to explain that we need what Alistair Cockburn calls *A Methodology Per Project*.[85] The state of the art is such that we need to allow development teams to pick the appropriate methodology based on the specific circumstances of their projects. The challenges and problems of each project demand a certain *requisite variety* from the development process. If the process cannot respond, then the project will go out of control.

We Need to Break Away from the Software Engineering Waterfall Process

Incremental development works. Business users actually prefer it, because it is easier for them to check a partial application than to validate a set of design documentation. It makes progress visible and concrete in a way that plans and documentation cannot. As anyone who has ever had a house built will attest, you typically visit the house every week (or more often); if nothing looks different from one visit to the next, you get worried. With the waterfall approach, it is easy to consume half of the available time before anything can be demonstrated to the users, let alone producing something that the users could try out usefully. Interestingly, this type of incremental development was understood by Fred Brooks when he wrote *The Mythical Man-Month:* "One always has, at every

---

85. http://members.aol.com/humansandt/papers/methyperproject/methyperproject.htm.

stage in the process, a working system. I find that teams can grow much more complex entities in four months than they can build."

The state of the art of software development is such that we practically have to do incremental, evolutionary development. It is possible to accomplish all of the requirements capture, followed by all of the design, and then all of the coding, but this waterfall approach, although endemic in the industry, is risky and fraught with problems. For any reader who doubts that the waterfall mindset is still fully in control, ask yourself whether status and pay are higher in the jobs at the top of the waterfall and lower in the downstream positions. Few companies pay testers or maintenance programmers as much as business analysts or systems analysts (note that these job titles are easily slotted into the waterfall model as well).

The Waterfall Approach Is Hazardous Because It Requires a Large Team

With the strict phasing of activities in the waterfall process, communication between specialists occurs through formal documents. Because a systems analyst cannot assume that the designer assigned to the project will understand anything about the problem domain, the requirements documentation must be "as complete as possible." As the analyst learns more about the project as time progresses, she has increasingly more to write. The fun really starts when the requirements change, and the analyst has to check several hundred pages of documentation to see what is affected. Small wonder, then, that smaller teams using this process get stuck in *analysis paralysis*.

Changes have to be communicated downstream so software engineering has to worry about requirements traceability. This effort makes it possible to communicate the effects of every change to the designers. In turn, the designers must discover the impact of the change on their designs, make any necessary changes, and communicate these changes to the programmers. Similarly, the testers and user documentation writers need to be informed and work out how the changes affect them. Small wonder that participants in waterfall projects complain about the high cost of change and try to "freeze" requirements.

Such issues do not present a problem in a true software engineering project where resources are effectively unlimited. It is a different story for a resource-constrained commercial project, however.

Two or more years into a project, the users may realize that they have spent a lot of money and have nothing useful to show for it. Some projects are lucky enough to salvage something from this effort, while others are unlucky enough to get reported as horrible examples of what can happen if a project does not use accepted software engineering practices.

Small Teams Should Never Attempt to Use a Software Engineering Approach

Software engineering works to the extent that you can, as they say in the Land of Oz, "Pay no attention to the man behind the curtain." As long as you are not resource-constrained, software engineering is an effective approach to software development. If your resource are limited, however, you cannot afford to throw hundreds of software engineers at the problem. You must recognize that software development is more of an intellectual, social task than it is a mechanical task. With that insight you can then learn many useful lessons from software engineering.

Chapter 16

Learning from Software Engineering

In learning from software engineering, we need to remain aware of the huge difference in scale among the projects being attempted. A large software craftsmanship project would take about 10 developer-years, whereas an extremely large application could take as many as 20 developer-years. Software engineering projects are 50 to 100 times larger, so they have to deal with different kinds of problems. Having said this, some of the problems are similar enough that useful lessons can be applied to software craftsmanship.

Size and Complexity Matter

Because communication inside large teams is an issue, early software engineering projects started to use subteams, with communication between these subteams being channeled through the senior developer. This *surgical or chief programmer team* approach gave dramatic productivity gains. Using chief programmer teams to reduce the need for communication inside the project is a practice that is firmly embedded in software craftsmanship. By using only especially capable developers, the craft approach drastically reduces the size of teams and hence the communication and coordination required. It also has practices in place to ensure that journeymen developers are encouraged to achieve mastery of the craft of software development.

In dealing with really large systems, the software engineering community learned that *modular decomposition* helps to reduce the overall complexity to a manageable level. By decomposing a system into loosely coupled modules, complexity is reduced and the modules can be worked on independently. This lesson has been applied very effectively in the Free Software/Open Source world. GNU Linux, for example, exploits the idea of modularity well, allowing the different modules to be developed completely independently. Software craftsmanship capitalizes on these ideas by focusing on creating small applications that work together to meet the needs of users. Rather than attempt to build really large, monolithic applications, the craft approach seeks to build small applications that can then build on and enhance each other.

Writing Applications Is Hard

A very early lesson from the software engineering community was that there is a big difference between writing small programs for yourself and developing systems for other people. This dichotomy has been variously described as programming in the small versus programming in the large[86] or the difference between a professional and an amateur programmer.[87] When developers write small programs, the programming task dominates all other activities; for applications and systems development, programming is merely a small portion of the overall effort. In larger software engineering projects, the requirements, verification, and validation activities dominate everything else. In the SAFEGUARD case mentioned in Chapter 1, more than 60% of the effort was related to understanding the requirements and then verifying that the solution actually satisfied those requirements. For the size of applications with which software craftsmanship deals, the shift is not as drastic—design and programming are the dominant activities. The problem of understanding the requirements and then verifying and validating

---

86. DeGrace, Peter, and L. H. Stahl, *Wicked Problems, Righteous Solutions*, Yourdon Press, 1990.

87. Weinberg, Gerald, *The Psychology of Computer Programming*, Dorset House, 1998.

the solution is much simpler because the users are involved in the development process.

Software craftsmanship adopts some of its ideas from *programming in the small* practices because the boundary between *small* and *large* is variable. With high-level, expressive programming languages and well-written code, good developers can keep the design of an entire application in their heads. Through the practice of having everyone on the team review all of the code as it is created and modified, the craft approach trains developers to hold increasingly larger designs in their heads. Hence the productivity penalty of *programming in the large* practices is incurred only for extremely large applications.

Applications Need to Be Well Structured

Applying the software engineering lessons of structured design and structured programming to software craftsmanship is really easy, because most modern programming languages were designed with these lessons in mind. Indeed, many modern programming languages have gone beyond structured programming and added object-oriented concepts as well. Java, Python, and Ruby are all relatively recent languages that have embraced the object-oriented paradigm and have become widely used for developing craft-sized applications. Python and Ruby were both developed in the Free Software/ Open Source tradition and have very active developer communities.

Change Can Be Expensive Unless You Allow for It

The lessons from the software engineering community about the effects and cost of change are interesting. The simplest lesson is that changing the hardware or programming language in the middle of a project is risky and expensive. Applying this idea to a typical three- to six-month craft project means that you have to pick the tools and technology very early in the life of a project. A secondary lesson is that changing the programming language or hardware is possible, so a project should do so if necessary.

The inevitability of change is a related lesson. Hardware changes, compilers change, software tools change. Although projects can survive these changes, making changes toward the end of a project is very risky. Every change to the underlying technology breaks something in the application, so craft projects should adopt the software engineering idea of having "freeze dates," after which certain kinds of change are deferred until critical milestones are reached.

Software engineering also teaches us that requirements are surprisingly volatile. Capers Jones[88] suggests that 1% to 2% of requirements change per calendar month or project duration. The craftsmanship approach takes this to heart by using incremental development and evolutionary delivery, with projects typically lasting between three and nine months. The reason is that requirements changes are expensive only prior to delivery, when their effects on the rest of the work in progress must be assessed. Once an application is live, requirements changes are much simpler to handle, as customers and users can point to the application and show what needs to be different. This approach is much easier than having to read all of the requirements and design documentation to see whether it has been affected by the requested change.

Software craftsmanship projects have a much lower cost of change than we would predict from software engineering projects. Rapid delivery means that requirements changes are less likely before the application goes live. After the application is live, changes are made with reference to the application, not the requirements documents. So unlike software engineering projects, craft projects do not need to incur the expense of maintaining requirements traceability. It's cheaper to take the low risk of having to scan through the application for the impact of a change than it is to slow a craft project down by insisting on complete requirements traceability. For software engineering projects, the trade-off is exactly the opposite: Traceability is necessary because it would be very expensive to check over the entire requirements and design documentation for the impact of a change.

---

88. Jones, Capers, *Assessment and Control of Software Risks,* Prentice-Hall, 1994.

Communication Inside the Team and with Users Is Crucial

A closely related lesson from software engineering is that multisite development is more difficult than single-site development because of the more restricted communication between remote sites. Large software engineering projects must deal with this problem, but software craftsmanship can bypass it by choosing to co-locate the entire team. After all, it is easy to make sure that a team of ten people can be situated next to each other. Putting the development team next to its users would similarly improve communication about requirements, so it is probably advisable for applications with complex requirements to do so.

If co-location is impossible for your project, as it often is for truly global projects, you need to pay special attention to communication. Fancy technology solutions such as videoconferencing might sound attractive, but time zone differences can soon make such options impractical.

The key thing to remember is that craftsmanship is personal. Make sure that you take the time to gather people together so that they can get to know one another. Although travel costs may be high, they will be offset by fewer misunderstandings and much smoother communication when people return to their normal locations. Even traditional requirements specifications are easier to read and understand when you know the person who wrote the document.

Documentation Is Always out of Date and Wrong

Another communication lesson from software engineering is that hardware and software never quite match their documentation. Sometimes it is just a case of developers using out-of-date documents; in other cases, the implementation just does not match the specification. On software engineering projects, this type of problem shows up when the hardware or software finally arrives and the design based on the documented behavior does not work properly. After much hunting for mistakes, the problem is often traced back to nonconforming hardware or supplied software.

Manage Risk Using Incremental Development

Software craftsmanship applies this lesson by using incremental development. A craft project front-loads uncertainty by developing the novel items early in the project. "Novel items" consists of those things that the team has never done before and new hardware/software with which the team does not have any experience. This schedule means that the team has time to deal with any surprises or can work around them without adversely affecting delivery.

Producing Accurate Estimates Is Very Expensive

A final lesson from software engineering is that a team has to do a lot of work on the requirements and ultimate design to reduce uncertainty on estimates. Initial project estimates made when only a high-level view of requirements exists can be off by as much as a factor of 4.[89] Once the main requirements have been identified, this estimate uncertainty can be reduced to a factor of 2. After all of the requirements have been described in detail, estimate uncertainty can be reduced to a factor of 1.5. Only after all of the detail design work has been completed, however, is it possible to reduce estimate uncertainty to a factor of 1.25 or less. Using the SAFEGUARD numbers as an example, a software engineering project would need 20% of its time and budget to get an estimate within 50%. To lower this uncertainty to 25% would take as much as 40% of the overall effort and duration. The SAFEGUARD project needed to expand more than 2,000-staff years before it could create an estimate to the nearest 1,000 staff-years.

Applying this estimating lesson to software craftsmanship is harder because the craft approach leverages itself from individual differences in ability. Although, in very large teams, individual differences average out, on a small team you have to know the team members before you can estimate. It is possible to produce a ballpark estimate early in a project, but unless the team has already worked on a similar project, this estimate could be off by a factor of 4.

---

89. Boehm, Barry W., *Software Engineering Economics*, Prentice-Hall, 1981.

For some projects, it is sufficient to get an order of magnitude estimate—for example, 4 calendar months, 2 developer-years versus 18 calendar months, 20 developer-years. Some customers and managers, however, are uncomfortable with wide ranges on estimates. In those cases, it is necessary to spend time and effort at the start of a project to refine the estimates further. Luckily, most of the work needed to create refined estimates is also work that has to be done to develop the application anyway. Nevertheless, the lesson of software engineering is that getting better estimates takes significant time and effort.

The most challenging part of the estimating lesson from software engineering is that customers and managers do not want to believe the initial estimates. It is as if the "sticker shock" of seeing the initial estimate pushes people into negotiating mode. Despite the evidence that the estimate is an outcome of the project parameters, customers and managers seem to persist in believing that it is possible to negotiate for a lower estimate without changing the project parameters. The hard lesson from software engineering is that you can negotiate for a lower estimate, but the new estimate will be inaccurate. It is lower, but the project will still take as long as the original estimate (or sometimes longer, because in hurrying, the team might make mistakes). Craftsmen always have to negotiate on the project parameters and then report the effect that this has on the estimate. The strongest argument a craftsman has is her reputation for on-time delivery of robust, high-quality applications, and it is never worth blowing a reputation by shaving an estimate just to get a project.

Applying These Lessons to Software Craftsmanship

The last part of this book provides pragmatic advice for the establishment of software craftsmanship as a viable alternative to the software engineering culture. In doing so, it focuses on projects that, from the software engineering standpoint, are tiny (that is, projects that take fewer than 10 developer-years). Indeed, much of what follows is aimed at application projects that take fewer than 12 developer-months.

PART 5

What to Do on Monday Morning

What can we take from software craftsmanship to improve the way that we deliver software right now? Of course, by asking that question, I am asking for a quick-fix solution that is in many ways incompatible with the ideas of craftsmanship, but practical action has always been the hallmark of a craftsman. To make a lasting improvement to the practice of software development, we need to address the systemic problem: Collectively we have been trying to tackle developing small applications the same way that we handle massive software engineering projects.

The final three chapters of this book address both the quick-fix and longer-term questions by covering three key topics: selecting developers for a project, establishing suitable design goals for application development, and empowering developers to become better at their craft. Each chapter begins with ideas that provide quick fixes that can have an immediate, beneficial impact on small application development projects. As each chapter progresses, the ideas presented may take longer to apply, but the potential impact and benefit from applying each idea is much greater. Toward the end of each chapter you might find that the ideas presented seem visionary and impractical; that will mean that I have achieved my goal of being deliberately provocative in introducing software craftsmanship.

Most of the ideas presented are personal-social in nature, as the real issues lie in that realm. Software engineering has given us good technical tools, but now the people side needs to be addressed to improve the effectiveness of software development.

With software craftsmanship, the intention is to get the best possible tools into the hands of capable developers so that small teams can create applications that once required the services of lots of people. Instead of accepting the software engineering challenge of finding 200,000 more developers, craftsmanship challenges us to find and empower 20,000 really good developers. It is not that we need to find more people. Rather, the real challenge is to make the developers we already have become much more effective. That is the real challenge for Monday morning—adopting software development practices that empower small teams to do really great work.

Chapter 17

Experience—The Best Indicator of Project Success

Although there have been few scientific studies, anecdotal evidence suggests that the best predictor of software delivery is experience. Unfortunately, not all experience is created equal. There is plenty of anecdotal evidence of the existence of developers who have 10 or 20 years of experience and who have, for one reason or another, failed to learn from that experience. This chapter mainly addresses the questions that customers and managers have when they attempt to find developers to create an application.

When it comes to delivering a project successfully, "Been there, done that, got the T-shirt" wins every time. That is, pick the developers whom you already know and trust. It is that simple. Software craftsmanship is built on top of long-term relationships that are grounded in a reputation for delivery.

For the absolute best chance of project success, choose a team that has just successfully delivered an application for you. Don't try to change anything, but just let the team start working on the next application.

Choose Software Craftsmen Based on Their Reputations

If you don't have a complete team handy, then choose the best software craftsman you know—the person with the best reputation for delivering great applications. A word of caution: This does not mean shopping the search out to a "body shop." It means searching your own memory for software craftsmen who have created great applications for *you*. Remember, craftsmanship is personal.

If none of these developers is available, see if you can postpone creating the application until he becomes available. Why delay starting? It is actually faster. When working with someone with whom you have previously worked, there is a shared understanding of what it takes to deliver great software. Even if you have to delay starting the project by six months, it is probably better to wait.

Trust the Craftsmen You Know to Recommend Other Craftsmen

Assuming that you don't want to wait until someone you know and trust becomes available, you need to extend the search. No, it is still not time to call the body shops. You also don't want to ask other managers or customers to recommend someone. Their recommendations are worthless because they have no skin in the game. If the person they recommend doesn't work out, they may say "sorry," but that apology will not fix the problem.

The people you want to ask are the craftsmen you want but cannot get. Ask them who they would *personally recommend* to create the application for you. By making it personal, you are asking them to stake their reputations on the successful delivery of that application by the craftsmen they recommend. You must be very careful not to push for an answer, however. That is, you must be really clear that it is OK if they do not know anyone whom they could recommend. If you push for a name, you are letting them off the hook; they are no longer responsible for the project outcome. By insisting on recommendations, you have lowered the quality threshold and basically have insisted on being given names regardless of how good they are.

If you are given a name, have the craftsman you know set up a meeting for all three of you. A three-way meeting emphasizes to both craftsmen that both of their reputations are at stake. Having all three of you in the same place at the same time makes it personal.

If Personal Recommendation Fails, Conduct a Wide Search

If no names emerge from personal recommendations, you should think long and hard about whether it is possible to delay the project. Anyone you locate at this point will be an unknown quantity from your organization's standpoint. When you ask for help this time, you are not asking for recommendations. Ask for craftsmen who have developed similar applications using the same technology. If you cannot find any people who match this criterion, widen your search to include craftsmen who have developed similar applications or have delivered systems using the same technology that your application will use. Then pick the best-qualified candidates from both categories—some who know the application and some who know the technolo

Evaluate Craftsmen Based on Their Reputations and Portfolio

At this stage of the search, you are looking for only one person—a software craftsman whom you can trust to deliver your application. Assembling the rest of the development team is the responsibility of the craftsman. After all, you can scarcely expect a craftsman to put his reputation on the line if he has no control over the quality of the development team.

The first thing to check is a craftsman's reputation. This is when you need to ask managers and customers for their recommendations and what they know about the available candidates. At this stage you are basically trying to assess whether you can trust the craftsman to lead the project. This consideration is less about technical qualifications and more about reputation, maturity, and attitude.

Carefully Examine a Craftsman's Portfolio

Assuming that a craftsman's reputation checks out, the next thing to check is his portfolio of applications. You need to have a lot of due diligence at this stage. If you are not technically strong, get a craftsman you trust to help you out. Talk to the managers, customers, and users of the applications in the craftsman's portfolio. Push for details and concrete examples, as you will need this information when you give the craftsman an audition.

When reviewing the portfolio, you are looking for evidence of success on similar-sized projects. One lesson from software engineering is that different-sized projects need different processes. A craftsman with a great track record in delivering small applications in small, one to six person-month projects might not be successful with a ten person-year project. Going from working with one or two people to working with ten or more team members is a challenge. Scaling up the size of the project by a factor or 20 or more is a challenge. For this reason, you should choose a craftsman who has a reputation for completing similar-sized projects.

I've lost count of how many times I've seen projects flounder from this mismatch. It's difficult to handle projects that are much larger or much smaller than the size with which you normally deal. Yes, it is possible to make the change, but you have to be aware that the rhythm of the project will be a whole lot different and that it will feel like everyone else is doing things wrong until you get used to the new size.

Auditioning a Software Craftsman

Forget all of the interviewing games you have ever heard of. The craftsman is auditioning for the lead role in the project. Pick your best candidate and give that person lots of background information about the project. Give the candidate time to prepare and then bring her in for a half- or whole-day audition. Make sure that all of the key players in the project are present for this audition. If this effort is successful, it is actually the kick-off meeting for the project.

By the end of the day you will know whether you have picked the right person. If the individual came well prepared, had thought about the application, asked the right questions, listened to the answers, and contributed to the discussion, she is probably a good choice. In the end, though, it is more about feel. How do you feel about working closely with this person for the next 12 months or however long the application will take?

Once you have made your decision, let everyone know immediately. Even if you are only ten minutes into the audition, it's OK for someone to shout "Next!" The basic rule is that if the audition is still running at the end of the day, you hire the person then and there.

No games. No seeing whether the next candidate might be more suitable. Once you find someone with whom you can work, you have completed the selection process. You must still sort out the contract and financial details, but those are just legal formalities. You have chosen a software craftsman to create your application.

Let Your Software Craftsman Pick the Rest of the Development Team

Picking the rest of the development team is the craftsman's responsibility. Although the manager and customer have to agree to the final team, they must also trust the choices made by the craftsman. If they do not trust the team that is assembled, it is a clear signal that the wrong craftsman was chosen. Correct that mistake by disbanding the team and starting the search for a new craftsman.

The Craftsman Should Pick the Team Based on Personal Knowledge and Recommendations

Developers who have worked together successfully in the past tend to be very productive as part of the same team. Craftsmen use this knowledge when selecting their team. Indeed, they will probably know who they want to use when they come for the audition. They want to keep their team intact. A *jelled team* can be hyperproductive compared with a non-jelled team.[90] One of the goals of software craftsmanship is to form hyperproductive small teams that can create robust, high-quality applications. If achieving that goal means that the existing team has more say in the selection decisions than is normal in an organization, so what? The goal here is effective delivery of software applications. If that goal is valuable to an organization, then making a minor change to policy is a small price to pay.

The Development Team Should Be "Experience Heavy"

Small teams have no space for "warm bodies" and have only a little space for beginners. Warm bodies are a liability in small teams

---

90. DeMarco, Tom, and Timothy Lister, *Peopleware*, 2nd edition, Dorset House, 1999.

because their resistance to change drags everybody else down. Enthusiastic beginners are a welcome addition to a small team, but if more than one-third of the team falls into this category, you have what Alistair Cockburn calls the "day-care pattern." You have a "training team," not a "delivery team."[91] Of course, it can be useful to run a training team to bring a group of trainees up to speed relatively quickly, but the focus of a training team is to get the team members trained (not to develop your application).

By making sure that your team is "experience heavy," you enable the experienced developers to focus on developing the application. You encourage everyone to play at the top of his game and create an environment in which one or two beginners can be coached and supported. Although there might be some corporate pressure for your team to "share some of the experience around," that would be counterproductive.

When good developers work together, their combined productivity is much higher than when they work alone. Working with beginners really slows good developers down, so a team of four beginners and one good developer is probably less productive than the good developer working alone. In start-ups, for example, the founders often get the first version up and running in a few months; they then hire a load of cheap developers to get the next release out, which takes forever to produce. Please do not inflict this problem on yourself.

Be Very Afraid of Low-Budget Teams

One really good developer is more valuable to your project than five average developers. When figuring out what you can afford to pay, think about the costs that may be incurred or the opportunities lost if the application is delivered late. It is good practice to reward exceptionally productive developers, because they make the difference between success and failure. Culturally, this type of reward system can be really hard to do in large corporations because someone might complain that you are paying the developer too much. Guess what? That hesitancy is why large corporations are now struggling to attract good developers.

---

91. Cockburn, *Surviving Object Oriented Projects*.

Collaborative Development

Once you have a great team of experienced developers, you need to match them up with experienced users. Success in software development depends on understanding the problem domain just as much as it does understanding the technology. Selecting the users on the team is just as important as selecting the developers.

Software craftsmen need demanding users who will play an active role in the development process. Their presence ensures that domain knowledge is available to the development team all of the time. Without this active involvement, development is slower and less efficient. Lack of user involvement is a great way to slow a team down by forcing team members to wait for information and decisions. It makes the team less efficient because reviews and feedback are delayed.

Use Incremental Development to Keep the Application on Track

Software craftsmanship implies an incremental development process. By using an incremental requirements capture process, you can develop the application incrementally, always ensuring, at each step of the way, that the users and customer give feedback.

This feedback has to be frequent and immediate. If the developers receive user feedback two weeks after they create a screen, chances are that a lot of rework will be required. By collaboratively developing a screen, user feedback is immediate, and rework is minimized. By staying involved, the users are in a better position to steer the application in the desired direction.

It is a real mistake for a user to let a developer work on something for more than a day without providing feedback. Similarly, it is a real mistake for a developer to let a user postpone looking at something for more than a day. Both mistakes are like driving down a highway with your eyes closed. Sooner or later, you need to do a panic course correction. Everybody has to keep her eyes open and stay part of the conversation to deliver robust, high-quality applications.

Deal with Mistakes in Team Selection as Early as Possible

Some developers do not like collaborative development. They prefer to work alone and to show their work to users only when the application is complete. Other developers cannot handle the incremental requirements part of incremental development. These individuals prefer to have a complete requirements specification before starting design work. Other developers cannot handle a team environment. Still others are cynical individuals who cannot handle actively learning and staying up-to-date with new ideas. All of these problems (and more) can destroy the effectiveness of collaborative development.

As soon as anyone on the team even begins to suspect that the team might be falling prey to one of these problems, it is important to bring the problem out into the open. Talk about the issues and coach the affected individuals. If the behavior doesn't change very quickly, remove those individuals from the project team. It is much better to have a great team that is slightly understaffed than it is to have a fully staffed, but sick team. A healthy team is always much more effective.

Anyone Can Learn to Do Collaborative Development

A perennial argument against collaborative development is that developers are geeks and all geeks are introverts. How can you expect an introvert to work collaboratively? How can you expect geeks to communicate? I can and I do.

Developers are not expected to turn into extroverts. They *are* expected to do what they excel at—namely, show their colleagues what they are working on; look at what their colleagues are doing to see what they can learn; spot as many loopholes, flaws, and mistakes as possible; ask what other features are needed in an application; and demonstrate those features that they have added. Not even the most introverted geek will find this requirement hard in a small team of people they know and trust. All it takes is some time to get to know all the members of the team, and having a small team makes this easier.

Avoid Bleeding-Edge Technology
If At All Possible

What is bleeding-edge technology? Any technology that is new to the team. If no one on the team has delivered a comparable-sized application using the technology, you are in bleeding-edge territory.

Think long and hard about why you want to use that technology before proceeding. It may look good on a résumé, but it also exposes the project to a very high risk of technical failure.

If there are sound commercial reasons for using the technology, then give the team plenty of time to explore it. In such a case, you should use a really experience-heavy team, where the team has experience in a very wide range of technologies.

You will also want to overstaff the quality assurance and testing sides of the development team. Bleeding-edge technologies are great sources of subtle mistakes and errors. To avoid major problems later, the development team must spend time early in the project trying to find all of the surprises, traps, and pitfalls. Having really experienced quality assurance and testing personnel on the team can help with this issue.

Paying for Experience

Once you have found some good developers, the question then becomes, "How do we ensure that we retain experienced staff?" The answer: by demonstrating that you value them. Use the standard organizational means of showing how valued a person is—pay that individual well.[92] I don't mean that you should pay them slightly above average, but a truly great developer is worth at least as much as any manager (including the CEO). This compensation plan may be hard to get past the various corporate policy guidelines, but higher pay is the most effective of all of the recommendations in this chapter.

Right now, barring winning big in the entrepreneurial start-up game, software developers have to move into another field if they are really ambitious. There is no incentive to stick around because, salarywise, software developers hit the top of the allowable bands very quickly. Once a developer reaches that point, the only way to

---

92. Although one reviewer pointed out that studies show that compensation is far down the list when it comes to retaining staff, here I mean retaining people in software development, not just in an organization. Many great developers choose to move out of software development because managing developers pays more than developing software.

advance is to jump ship for a different organization. Organizational policies actively discourage the retention of skilled experienced staff because they do not effectively reward productive developers.

Where Are All the Great Developers of Yesteryear?

Although much great software was written in the 1970s and 1980s, few of those developers are still actively developing software. Most have moved on to other activities that provide greater rewards. Although many remain involved in the software industry, they are no longer developers. Instead, they had to become managers, entrepreneurs, or researchers to advance. Some have opted out of the field entirely and have joined the academic world.

This is crazy. What incentive is there for someone to excel at software development if, by the time the person has learned how to do it well, he must find an alternate career? Even start-ups make this mistake. The founders create some great software, get the company off the ground, and then move into management. They then hire a bunch of beginners to mess up their software.

Rewarding Great Developers

Attracting and keeping really great developers is a problem for most organizations. They find it problematic because they go about the process totally wrong.

Some companies try to use stock options to compensate developers, but this policy doesn't address the fundamental problem. Organizations continue to make the mistake of rewarding managers more handsomely than great developers. Look at any company. Who gets the best stock options? It surely isn't the developers. Imagine how long a professional sports team would last if the coach was paid more than the star players.

To get around organizational salary bands that restrict how much a great developer can be paid, many projects opt to use contract staff because contractors can be paid three or four times what employees receive. This approach is a mistake because it fails to reward experience. An employee who has worked for an organization for ten years is much more valuable than an outsider because of his detailed, indepth domain knowledge. On a project, employees will waste time teaching the high-paid contractors about the business. Very soon the entrepreneurial employees will decide to become contractors, and the organization will lose all of its knowledge and expertise.

If you plan to use contractors, make sure that they are really great developers. Your employees must think that working with these outsiders is a great opportunity. They have to be learning lots about software development during the experience. They have to be amazed at how fast the application is created and how great it is. They must also see that they cannot compete and hence won't try to become a contractor.

If You Want Great Developers, You Have to Pay Them Well

I've said this before and I will repeat it now. You have to realize that it's OK to pay good employees as much as, or more than, they would receive as independent contractors. If a good developer is as productive as ten average developers, it's just good sense to pay her as much as ten average developers—after all, that is the employee's replacement cost.

For most organizations, this issue is a showstopper. Corporate policies put a ludicrously low ceiling on developer salaries. Hopefully, you will get those policies changed in time to help your projects.

But How Can We Afford to Pay for the Great Developers?

Simple. Stop overpaying average developers. A developer with only two years experience is not worth $40,000 to $60,000 per year, even if Java does appear on his résumé. Most teams that are assembled are far too inexperienced; that is, they are experience light, not experience heavy.

For your next project, forget about assembling a team of 10 or 15 beginners. Instead, have a really great developer pick one or two other great developers to help deliver the application. Let that team pick one or two apprentices or journeymen to assist them. Now make the great developers an offer they cannot resist. Sign them up for a two- or three-year renewable contract for an outrageous salary to deliver great applications. Pay them at least $150,000 per year, and possibly pay more than $250,000 per year for a truly outstanding developer. You will still save money compared with hiring a team of ten average developers. For that price you should be able to entice good, independent contractors to become salaried employees.

Once this team is in place, make it clear that you expect robust, high-quality applications that can be maintained and enhanced for years. Let the team members know that they have not been hired to complete a specific project, but rather to create, support, and enhance an application that meets a business need. Establish the expectation that it is not acceptable to move on when they feel like it; if team members want to move on, they must train a successor first. Let them know that you expect the team to stay intact for at least ten years and that the applications they create should last even longer.

Be Prepared to Be Amazed

If you can manage to create a small team of great developers, you will be amazed at the results. To see what is possible, consider Jim Coplien's report on Borland software craftsmanship, which describes the team that built Quattro Pro for Windows:

> *The initial QPW development team comprised highly productive professionals who viewed each other with the highest respect. These perhaps sound like hollow words that most managers would apply to their organizations, until one looks more deeply into what "highly productive" and "respect" mean.*

> *The QPW development team has chronologically mature membership by industry standards. "We have professionals, not hired guns," noted one member of the development team. People are brought into the team for their recognized expertise in domains of central importance to the project: spreadsheet engines, graphics, databases, and so forth. No one is viewed as a warm body or general engineer or interchangeable employee: Each brings special talents to the effort.*

> *QPW had a small core team—four people—who interacted intensely over two years to produce the bulk of the product.*

> *One widely held stereotype of companies that build PC products (or of California-based companies) is that they hire "hackers" and that their software is magic, unreadable spaghetti. Meeting with this group broke that stereotype for me. Their constant attention to architectural issues, their efforts to build an evolvable structure, their care to document the system well (both externally and internally) are all hallmarks of the highest professionalism. Those attitudes, coupled with the phenomenal general-purpose programming talents of the staff, plus the high level of domain-specific expertise,*

defined the kind of quality value system necessary to an effective and productive process. There were few gratuitous shortcuts and few novice errors. From what I saw, these people produce very high quality code.[93]

The most telling part of the report is the amazing productivity of the team:

The project assimilated requirements, completed design and implementation of 1 million lines of code, and completed testing in 31 months. Coding was done by no more than eight people at a time, which means that individual coding productivity was higher than 1000 lines of code per staff-week. . . . Analyses of the development process are "off the charts" relative to most other processes we have studied.[94]

This is the promise of software craftsmanship—the creation of small, hyperproductive development teams that can create amazing applications.

---

93. Coplien, James O., *Borland Software Craftsmanship: A New Look at Process, Quality and Productivity*, www.bell-labs.com/~cope/Patterns/Process/QPW/ borland.html.

94. Coplien, *Borland Software Craftsmanship*.

Chapter 18

Design for Testing and Maintenance

Software is long-lived. Even simple throwaway applications have proved to be hard to turn off. If an application is both usable and useful, it tends to be used and extended for years. As developers we need to take this longevity into account. The best way to do so is to lose the project mindset and treat *software as capital.*[95] Regardless of what accounting guidelines are in place, software applications are capital assets, and replacing them requires a lot of expense and work.

Software craftsmanship seeks to maximize the useful life of applications because the costs and risks involved in replacing them are immense. First, consider the cost of the development project itself, which in most cases is nontrivial. Second, data conversion and changeover costs arise. Finally, there are the retraining costs for the staff who use the application. These retraining costs can be really significant for applications, especially when in-house training courses are required to teach users how to use the application.

---

95. Baetjer, *Software as Capital.*

Think Applications, Not Projects

Switching from a project-based approach to an application lifetime-based approach is something that is relatively simple, yet it has profound implications. Moving away from projects changes the time horizon used when making decisions and, in doing so, addresses many of the problems associated with short-term thinking. In thinking about the overall lifetime of an application, we have a practical way of talking about incremental development and evolutionary delivery. Rather than burdening a project with everything that customers and users can possibly imagine, an application mindset allows for steady incremental improvement over time.

Applications Are Never Finished, Only Retired

An application mindset smoothes out the demand for development resources, because rather than offering the drastically fluctuating demands of crash projects, applications present a steady demand. Initially, a small team of developers creates the first release of an application. They then continue to work on the application by delivering more features, improvements, and enhancements as well as fixing any mistakes. Eventually, the developers and users come to realize that the application will never be "finished," that they are collaboratively evolving the application to meet the needs of the business, and that there is no reason for that evolution to cease.

This realization is a key theme in software craftsmanship. Applications are long-lived and can easily outlast their creators, provided that we pay attention to this possibility when we first create them. Software craftsmanship does so by making sure that developers are aware that creating orphan applications is bad for one's reputation. It also holds developers responsible for the maintenance and enhancement of their applications until they find a worthy successor to look after these applications. Thus developers know that they are going to have to maintain the applications they create. As a result, they pay attention to the long-term health of the code. The need to find a worthy successor to take over the maintenance of the application similarly forces a developer to be careful because no one will be eager to take on the maintenance of a messy application.

Maintenance Teams Should Refuse to Accept Bad Applications

Today, you probably employ some sort of hand-off from the development team to a maintenance team. That is, at the end of the typical software engineering project, the developers shift responsibility for the application to the maintenance team. Regardless of the state of the application, the maintenance team probably cannot turn down a badly written, unmaintainable application. The craft approach improves this situation by changing the status of maintenance, so that any developer can refuse to take over the maintenance of badly written applications.

Maintainable Applications Need Automated Tests

A simple change that can be made relatively easily and that will improve application maintainability is to encourage developers to create automated tests for their applications. By doing this, developers protect themselves from the effects of trivial mistakes, which are easy to make when changing applications. By having an automated regression test, a developer can be relatively confident that her changes have not broken anything.

Although errors may initially slip by the automated regression tests, as long as developers continue to beef up the regression test suite every time a problem occurs, eventually the regression tests become a very good safety net. Effectively, the regression test suite detects all known mistakes in the application, so only new kinds of mistakes can slip through. This type of test is a real boon when it comes to maintenance. When developers fix one problem, they fear that they are introducing or uncovering another problem. Having a test suite that can be run with very little manual effort takes a lot of the stress out of maintenance.

Start Making Your Applications Testable

Just as the engineering world can do *design for manufacture*, software developers can do *design for testing*. Design for testing is better, however, because it creates maintainable software. In contrast, design for manufacture results in large components that have to be thrown away when a small item breaks. Design for testing discourages the creation of badly coupled code and encourages appropriate decomposition into cohesive modules. Indeed, object-oriented designs are especially sensitive to this effect. It is practically impossible to create good regression tests for badly coupled, object-oriented designs and really easy to create good regression tests for object-oriented designs that minimize unnecessary coupling. Kent Beck and Erich Gamma popularized this concept with their JUnit[96] testing framework, which has now been replicated in many programming languages. Few developers who have experienced the power of JUnit ever want to go back to programming without it or its equivalent.

Design for testing is important because, as systems become more interconnected and interdependent, validating a new configuration becomes increasingly more important. If verification is cheap, then we can afford to do it after every change. If it is expensive or difficult, then the natural temptation is to skimp on the verification work for "simple" changes. This path leads to lower-reliability systems, something that we are starting to see happening.

Design for Maintenance

There are two competing strategies for creating maintainable applications. The first strategy is to design configurable systems that have the necessary flexibility designed up front to cater for foreseen changes. The ultimate aim of this strategy is to create a system that is so configurable that most changes can be accomplished without having to change the application code.

The second strategy is to create simple systems so that it is a relatively quick and easy process to change the application to meet the changing requirements. The aim of this strategy is to defer investing in flexibility until there is definitive proof that the flexibility is necessary and cannot easily be accommodated just by changing the application.

The Design for Maintenance workshop at OOPSLA 1999[97] concluded that both of these strategies can reduce maintenance costs;

---

96. JUnit can be downloaded from www.junit.org.

97. http://www.mcbreen.ab.ca/oopsla99/DesignForMaintenanceWorkshop.html.

most projects do neither. That is, they fail to spend enough time investigating the problem domain to be able to identify the necessary flexibility and configurability, and they fail to create a simple, easy-to-change application. Instead, the project tries to follow the middle ground and, in the process, increases the overall cost of maintenance. Please avoid this trap. If you are going to build in flexibility, make sure that it will be needed. If you cannot predict how much flexibility will be needed, then make the application as easy to change as possible—after all, you will undoubtedly have to change it somewhere.

Experienced Developers Are Needed to Create Maintainable Applications

There are no easy answers to the problem of finding out whether doing more analysis will reduce risk. In some cases, it pays to do more analysis because eventually the underlying domain, although very complex, is understandable. In others, more analysis will not help because the underlying domain is complex and emergent. It is not something to be understood, only something to be created. You need experienced developers to tell these two cases apart.

Maintainable Applications Can Last for a Very Long Time

With very long-lived applications, it is impossible to predict all possible changes, so it might be preferable to adopt a simple design approach initially. Because we probably cannot design all of the necessary flexibility up front to cater for all eventualities, we must instead design systems that are easy to modify, enhance, and fix. As the necessary flexibility later becomes evident, we can rework the application to add the necessary configuration features. This approach defers the cost of making the application flexible until the point where it would cost more to continue to make small changes in the same area.

Long-Lived Applications Require Long-Lived Development Tools

A key question that needs to be asked when considering long-lived applications is whether your development tools are likely to remain stable for the lifetime of the application. This question can be really tough to answer, but we need to start thinking about it because the 1990s were littered with tools that have not survived. How would you act differently if your users insisted that the application has to be usable for the next 20 years, just like any other capital asset?

First, you would pick a programming language that would be around in substantially the same form in 20 years. Next, you would ensure that any platform-dependent code was well encapsulated so that it could be replaced with an alternate implementation.

Software Craftsmen Prefer Nonproprietary, Open Source Tools

Choosing a programming language has always been a difficult problem. Single vendor and new languages are always risky, because the single vendor may fail or the language might not catch on. I prefer to pick languages that have existed for more than ten years and/or languages that are Free Software/Open Source platforms. If a language has survived for ten years, there is probably a healthy user community that will ensure its ongoing support or, failing that, an incentive for the creation of a viable migration path. Free Software/Open Source languages are an option because, if all else fails, the source is available, and someone else can be enticed into taking over support.

Java Is Hazardous to the Health of Your Projects

Java, which is currently the most hyped programming language, fails to make the cut under these criteria. It's too new and it's proprietary. Does that mean that it shouldn't be used? No, but it does mean that it should be used only if the planned life of the application is relatively short—definitely less than five years. As yet, Java does not have the track record for stability that other programming languages have. Although there is a lot of marketing momentum behind Java right now, until a defined and stable standard emerges, it is a high-risk option compared with standardized languages.

Maintainable Applications Need a Stable Infrastructure

As well as a stable programming language, long-lived applications need a stable infrastructure. Unfortunately, we know that goal isn't really feasible, so we have to settle for encapsulating the platform-dependent code. For applications, three parts of the infrastructure need to be encapsulated: the user interface, the database, and the operating system.

If we take the operating system first, by and large, this problem has been solved. Most programming languages have a relatively portable way of accessing the system services of the underlying operating system. Writing portable applications that can run on many different operating systems, although still difficult, is not impossible.

Insulating your application from the underlying database is not getting much easier. Despite attempts at standardizing Structured Query Language (SQL), the database world seems to be reinforcing the old joke, "Standards are so good that everyone should have his own." Proprietary databases are a very lucrative business, and it is easy for an application to get locked into a particular vendor's technology. From the viewpoint of a 20-year application, however, tying your fate to that of a particular vendor is not a good idea. Relational databases have been viable for only 15 years, so who knows what database technology we will be using in ten years?

Database vendors are making it easier for an application to become dependent on a particular database technology by promoting stored procedures and similar ideas. That practice encourages developers to write application logic in a proprietary programming language inside the database. Although it can make the application run faster, the real effect is to make it practically impossible to port the application to a different database. For long-lived applications, you have to consider what the costs might be to deal with changes to the vendor's proprietary language or to move the application to a different database in the future.

Insulating your application from the user interface is probably the hardest task of all. Over the years developers have had to deal with command-line and full-screen text interfaces, various graphical user interfaces, the Web, and now personal digital assistant (PDA) devices. Other technologies will certainly appear in the future, so the reality for most long-lived applications is that they must accommodate a variety of user interfaces.

Great Software Is Global

Internationalization (I18N) and multilingualization (M17N) will have a major effect on user interfaces in the future. It is no longer enough to provide an application in a single, Western language.

Instead, users are starting to need applications that can handle many different scripts and languages at the same time.

Although I've been aware of the internationalization issues for many years, I'd always thought that the solution was fairly simple—just translate the application into a different language. I've learned a lot since then, especially when I started to use Ruby, an object-oriented scripting language. Unlike most other programming languages, the really interesting documentation is written in Japanese. This fact should not be surprising given that the originator, Yukihiro Matsumoto (also known as Matz), is Japanese. Although there is an English home page for Ruby (http://www.ruby-lang.org/), there is also a Japanese home page (http://www.ruby-lang.org/ja/). My browser cannot handle the Japanese characters. Instead of showing the Japanese equivalent of "Ruby: A gem of a programming language," it shows something that is vaguely reminiscent of line noise, "$B%*%V%8%'%/%H;X8~%9%/%j%W%H8@8l(B Ruby."

Multilingualization is important because it will allow users to use whatever language and script they like and to mix and match languages at will. It is important for software craftsmanship because great software meets users' needs; it doesn't force all users to learn English.

Make Sure That Your Software Can Become Global

Unless developers do a good job of insulating an application from its user interface, they will need to do a lot of work to support the I18N and M17N initiatives. The flexibility to deal with different user interface styles and languages is easier to include when an application is initially designed. Although new user interfaces can be grafted on later, it is actually easy to determine whether an application needs this flexibility. If the application needs it, designing it up front is the sensible option from the design-for-maintenance viewpoint.

Insulating your application from the user interface requires that developers pay attention to detail and cleanly separate the user interface-specific code. Although a variety of cross-platform class libraries and user interface toolkits are available, none will help if a programmer embeds an English text string in the middle of the application code.

Software Craftsmen Need to Fight Back Against Planned Obsolescence

The combination of user interface, database, and operating system may make it harder for applications that are crafted today to last as long as they have in the past. In part, this short life results from the rapid evolution of the desktop PC environment, where it seems as if a "planned obsolescence" theme is at play. There is a tension between the needs of the shrink-wrapped software vendors, who need to be able to sell upgrades to "consumers," and the needs of organizations, which depend on applications to run their business. Vendors like change because it makes selling upgrades easier and because the cost of the extra development work is insignificant compared with the distribution and marketing effort. Business applications are different because the work of upgrading is a pure cost; it does not result in more sales revenue. Hence businesses tend to lag behind the consumer market in adopting new technologies.

Software craftsmen need to emphasize that it is possible to create applications that can last for long periods. Software does not have to be thrown away and replaced every few years.

Great Software Needs to Be Given a Great User Interface

From a software craftsmanship viewpoint, we need to start paying more attention to the usability of software and less attention to the surface glitter. Alan Cooper[98] uses the expression *putting lipstick on a pig* to refer to glittery graphical user interfaces pasted onto poorly designed applications. This problem is a design-for-maintenance issue because getting the basic user experience right means that there will be fewer demands for change in the future. It is also a problem of tool selection, as many proprietary tools specialize in producing flashy user interfaces with floating toolbars and animated icons that hide a pile of unmaintainable, badly designed code.

---

98. Cooper, Alan, *The Inmates Are Running the Asylum.*

Getting the user experience right is more than simply providing for ease of use or ease of learning. Applications are the ultimate adaptive power tool that can be adjusted to meet the needs of a user. Yes, users want ease of use, but they also desire power and productivity. As a user becomes more familiar with an application, effectiveness and efficiency become more important concerns. Although we have to allow for the novice user, an application that fails to cater to expert users will need to be replaced. Design for maintenance, then, means that we design applications that get out of the way of expert users, while allowing novices to use them safely.

Software Craftsmen Create Applications That Are Safe to Use

A parallel can be drawn between the tools that a software craftsman employs on a daily basis and the applications that users work with on a daily basis. The tools and applications place an upper bound on how effective a person can be in that role. No matter how clever the individual is, if the software gets in her way, it slows her down and makes her less effective. Just as developers prefer speed and the ability to automate routine tasks, users think that computers are supposed to make their daily tasks easier. The combination of software and skilled user is what matters, but users become skilled only if it is safe for them to experiment. Good software makes a user feel comfortable trying out new features, knowing that nothing will blow up if the "wrong" button is pressed.

Software craftsmen have a responsibility to make sure that there are no "wrong" buttons in an application. It is possible, after all, to create applications that are predictable and forgiving. This consideration is a design-for-maintenance issue because users who can safely explore and experiment will make fewer calls for support.

Maintainable Software Is Easy to Diagnose

Probably the major challenge when designing for testing and maintenance is to build sufficient diagnostics and instrumentation into an application. This task is difficult because few developers and managers understand how useful these tools are for supporting a live application. Good diagnostics make it possible to identify rapidly the causes of any failures. Good instrumentation makes it feasible to look inside the running application and observe how it is performing.

Developers come to appreciate these things only when they are responsible for the maintenance and support of live, performance-critical applications. Poorly formatted log files are just so much "spew":[99] What is really needed is an effective *test window* into the application (Hunt and Thomas suggest embedding a Web server as a way of seeing inside a running application). Although this window requires some work to create, for complex applications having some way of seeing what is happening inside the application is crucial for understanding the performance characteristics. Developers could use the operating system to see which resources an application is using, but that tactic is not nearly as useful as getting real numbers out of the application. It's the difference between saying "Yes, it does seem a bit slow today" and saying "Yes, the response time has stretched out to one second, but that's because we are doing lots more sales today." With detailed knowledge of what is happening in the application, developers are better able to handle support and maintenance work.

The Hazards of Outsourcing

Outsourcing is probably the opposite of design for maintenance. The ideal setup for project success is an experienced team that has worked together on similar applications, using your technology on similar-sized projects. So what are corporations doing instead? They are outsourcing application development to other companies. This approach practically guarantees that the "team" has never before worked together. You may have one or two experienced developers, but the rest will be relative beginners, and all will have to spend time learning your business and application domain.

Even worse, at the end of the project the team will be dispersed to other projects, and the detailed knowledge of how the application was built will be lost. Although you can ensure that the team document the application, we all know that this is insufficient. Despite the many programming books that have been written, companies still

---

99. Hunt, *The Pragmatic Programmer.*

make money training developers how to program; maybe if we could get the development team to write a training course on how to maintain and enhance the application, we would really get somewhere.

Creating an application brings with it the responsibility to support that application for as long as the users need it (and the customer is willing to pay for support). The original development team, therefore, has an obligation to train its successor and effect an orderly transition to the new team. Outsourcing breaks this pattern. It actively hinders the accumulation of experience about applications, because the outsourced development team will not maintain the application. The supplier may provide some level of support for your new application, but that support person will rarely be a member of the original team.

Outsourcing Ignores the Reality of Software Development

Outsourcing looks attractive from a scientific management point of view—it gives great revenue-to-employee ratios—but we all know *how to lie with statistics*. Outsourcing is a software engineering strategy that ignores the reality of software development. To be really effective, software developers need a deep knowledge of the application on which they are working. You can make outsourced projects work, but the software craftsmanship approach is much more effective.

If You Have to Use Outsourcing, Insist on a Software Craftsmanship Approach

If you are forced to use outsourcing, insist that your supplier commit to being involved for the planned life of the system—not just during the initial development project. Make sure that the supplier has a real economic incentive to retain the original development staff and make them available for maintenance and enhancements to your application. Maintaining contact with the original developers ensures that your application can be modified or enhanced quickly, without the delays and mistakes that typically occur when new developers try to work on an application. Allow the supplier to bring new developers into the maintenance team, but insist that they be brought in slowly and receive adequate supervision and training while they learn your application. Make sure that there are real economic disincentives for rapid turnover in the maintenance team.

Implementing these suggestions will impose restrictions on the supplier, but this is normal. In all fields that are high touch, and characterized by lots of tacit knowledge, we are normally very careful to ensure stability. Many people keep the same dentist, doctor, hairdresser, and lawyer for years; it is a real hassle to change because of the learning curve involved. The same is true in software development. Once you have found a team that you trust to develop the application, it is crazy to have them "hand off" that application to another team, because *applications are never finished.*

You Can Still Use Outside Craftsmen to Create Your Application

A safer alternative to outsourcing is to hire a craftsman and a development team to create an application on the condition that your people serve as apprentices on the project. Make it clear that the success of the project will be judged on how well your people can extend and enhance the application after the initial few releases. In this way, you make maintenance a priority during the initial development.

Ideally, you should give the craftsmen a series of applications to develop so that a long-term relationship is created. Keep the hybrid team of outside craftsmen and in-house apprentices intact. Over time, as your in-house staff learn and improve, you should plan for the passing of the baton from the outside craftsmen to your in-house journeymen.

Maintenance Is the Most Important Part of the Life of Any Application

Software engineering labeled the activities that take place after the initial release as "maintenance," but this terminology is really just a hangover from the mechanical metaphor. What is really going on here is a whole series of smaller software development projects—some fixing mistakes—but the bulk is either changing the application to meet changing business needs or making major functional enhancements to the application. This work should not be performed by a separate maintenance team. It is wasteful to train a new team of developers when you already have a team perfectly capable of doing this work.

Maintenance Needs to Be Made a High-Status Activity

Unlike software engineering, software craftsmanship values the people who maintain and enhance existing applications. As such, you do not need to maintain a separate maintenance team, because the original developers will stick around to look after an application. Craftsmen stick around until they find worthy successors because their reputations depend on their ability to create robust, high-quality applications. Their reputations will be damaged if they move on too quickly.

The reputations of craftsmen derive from the applications they have created and continue to support. No matter how good a developer is, creating an *orphan application* is not a good way to enhance one's reputation. An application is safe to use only if users know that it will continue to evolve and improve over time. Otherwise, users are gambling that no significant changes will occur in their business environment for as long as they need the application. Although they could try to find other developers to maintain the application, when developers know that they will not have to maintain an application, it is easy for them to slip into bad coding habits. We then see a string of applications being created because the previous ones were unmaintainable.

Craftsmen Have to Be Rewarded for Maintaining Applications

Organizations must provide an economic incentive for craftsmen to maintain their applications. After all, no one works for free. Keep the craftsmen on a retainer, give them related projects on which to work, or pay for the application continually to be enhanced and extended.

Whatever mechanism you use, your goal is the same—ensuring that the application stays up-to-date and integrated with all of your other applications. You never want to build up a large backlog of change requests against the application because that devalues the application. If you travel too far down that path, you will have another unmaintainable legacy application on your hands. The point of designing for maintenance is to ensure that applications can last for as long as they are needed.

Not All Software Has to Be Maintainable

Software always has to be testable, but sometimes it is OK to create a bleeding-edge application. New technologies can have a compelling competitive advantage that makes it worthwhile for a customer to accept the inherent cost penalties in being the first user of version 0.9 of a hot new development tool. As long as everyone understands the implications, it is possible to build great applications with new technology. Software craftsmen will, however, point out that they must test out the new technology thoroughly to identify any hidden traps or pitfalls. They will also point out that a year or two down the road the application will probably need to be rewritten, because as version 0.9 evolves into version 2.0, the original application will no longer work in the new environment.

If the new technology created a compelling competitive advantage, then the cost of this rewrite will not be an issue. It will be insignificant compared with the benefits that have accrued by having an innovative application. The challenge the software craftsmen face is one of keeping up with all of the evolving technology so that they can create high-quality, robust applications even when using bleeding-edge technologies.

Design for Testing and Maintenance Is Not Rocket Science

All good, experienced developers already know how to create maintainable applications. Craftsmen even like creating maintainable applications because doing so allows them to become very responsive to their users. Craftsmen enjoy being able to delight their users with the speed with which they can make changes. Creating testable, maintainable applications is simple, but unfortunately it is not easy.

Design for testing and maintenance requires an unusual depth and breadth of expertise in software development that can be gained only through years of practice and coaching. Although most developers know the relevant techniques (for example, ways to create loosely coupled, cohesive components with well-defined interfaces), few have taken the time to get really comfortable and familiar with these techniques. For this reason, software craftsmanship looks back to traditional apprenticeship as a means of giving beginners an adequate grounding and practice in the techniques.

Apprenticeship makes a difference because it instills a lifelong passion to master the craft. It instills a passion for perpetual learning and, in the process, enables the apprentice to become a great developer.

Chapter 19

Perpetual Learning

Software developers need to have a good memory, be very good at learning, and be great at forgetting. Forgetting is the most important ability because it is the key to perpetual learning. Learning is important because the field of software development is constantly evolving and changing. Every new application requires the developer to remember lots of new information and trivia. A key skill that developers need to master is the ability to forget the trivia while retaining the essential information.

Starting out on the journey of perpetual learning is simple. An easy and effective starting point is to provide each development team with its own small library of good technical books. *The Pragmatic Programmer* by Hunt and Thomas is an ideal starting point, and its recommendations about "building a library" are spot on.

Creating a Learning Environment

Once your developers have some books to read, the next step is to provide an environment in which they are encouraged to learn and apply what they have learned. If you have staffed your team with good, experienced developers, then you have already tackled most of this issue. Provide some time every week for your team members to goof off and learn something. Tell your developers to take one or two hours in the middle of every week to try out ideas that might improve their software development skills in a way that assists the current application. By routinely alloting time to focus on the craft of software development, you will find that developers' ability to deliver applications will improve.

You need to slot this learning time in the middle of the week because it puts some slack into the development process. Putting the learning time at the end of Friday afternoon is less effective because it leaves no time to put into practice what was learned. The ideal learning time is Tuesday or Wednesday morning, when everyone is back into the flow of work and enough time remains in the week to try out new ideas.

Use In-House Tutorials to Create a Learning Environment

If you haven't managed to staff your team with good, experienced developers, you will have to structure the learning time differently. Get your best developer to run a tutorial or study group for the rest of the team on immediately useful topics. Don't get too formal by trying to plan coverage of the topics weeks in advance. Trust the team to be able to identify what it needs on a week-by-week basis. What you are creating is "just-in-time" training delivery based on the immediate needs of the team.

Obviously, if the senior developer in the team cannot step up to this challenge, you might need to find someone outside the team to run the learning sessions. You might also want to ask whether someone else should lead the development team.

Invite Everyone to Present Seminars on Interesting Topics

Once you have the tutorials in place, start a series of seminars on wide-ranging topics. Invite everyone to take turns at introducing a topic of interest. These seminars offer a great way even for beginners to practice presenting technical topics. They also provide an extra incentive to study the topic in depth, as few people are comfortable presenting a topic until they know it well.

The Learning Time Is Time Invested in Process Improvement

Tutorials and seminars are a way of investing a small amount of time (less than 5%) every week to look for ways in which developers can improve their skills. It's a very small investment given the potential payback in increased productivity from having better developers on the team. Everyone on the development side, including the managers, should be involved in this learning time, because the attitude toward learning is the biggest differentiation between software craftsmanship and the software engineering mindset. Involving everyone sends a strong message to the entire organization. It demonstrates a commitment to the organization's people, allowing them to develop mastery in the craft of software development.

Mastering the Craft of Software Development

The software engineering mindset assumed that workers could be trained in the "one best way" to perform a task. Once they were trained, their job was to follow the process. Thinking was optional, and workers were expected to do everything in the way specified during their training. In contrast, with craftsmanship, the interaction between craftsmen, their growing mastery of the craft, and the application being created is dynamic. Apprentices initially learn the "one best way" to perform a task. As they progress in their understanding, they learn other, similar ways of doing the same task. By the time they have reached journeyman status, individuals have a deep understanding of how to choose the appropriate approach and are beginning to develop their own approaches. By the time they become master craftsmen, they should be able to create new approaches to a task whenever existing approaches appear suboptimal. Mastery has never been a case of finding the "one best way," but rather a journey of discovery in which new insights are possible, even in the most mundane of tasks.

In any community of practice, a key role for the journeymen is to surpass their masters, thereby moving the craft forward. This dynamic keeps all crafts refreshed and renewed. Rather than parroting the old masters, the journeymen task is to build on what the masters have created. This is why the tradition of the journeyman developed. After apprentices had learned all they could from one master, they would journey to work with other masters while they prepared to set themselves up as masters in their own right. In this manner, journeymen provided the necessary cross-fertilization of ideas between master craftsmen. Admittedly, the pace of diffusion was slow. Although conferences fulfill the same role today, we still need people to move the state of the art forward. By providing learning time every week, we create an environment in which mastery can flourish.

Encourage Participation in User Groups and Conferences

You should encourage your developers to get involved in local user groups and technical associations. Although the activities of these groups are inevitably less focused than your in-house learning time, they will introduce team members to new ideas outside their day-to-day field. Some of these new ideas may turn out to be applicable immediately and make a big difference in your work. Other ideas may not be immediately useful but may become feasible several years down the road. The rest of the ideas, although not directly applicable, will serve to keep the team actively learning and expanding their knowledge of software development.

Once or twice each year, you should send your developers to a relevant conference or training course. This policy demonstrates your commitment to perpetual learning. Without it, it is hard to convince developers, managers, customers, and users of the importance of allowing sufficient time for developers to keep their skills up-to-date. Although developers will continue learning on their own time as well, investing the organization's time sends a very clear message to everyone.

A training course is probably the best option for inexperienced staff, whereas conferences are probably better choices for more experienced staff. Few training courses are offered in an advanced and/or accelerated format that is suitable for good, experienced developers; rather, most training courses are targeted toward beginners and intermediates. Conferences, on the other hand, often assume a background that inexperienced developers do not have, making much of the conference inaccessible or of little value to them.

Choose Training Courses Very Carefully

When choosing training courses, make sure that your experienced developers check out the course and instructor to confirm that the course will be useful. That is, have your experienced developers read through the training materials and talk to the instructor to confirm for themselves the value of the course. Just looking at the syllabus or the list of topics covered is insufficient because it is the details that matter. If the training organization does not want to release the course notes for review, then that reluctance is a good indicator of the quality of the course and suggests that you should look for another training organization. Similarly if your experienced developers cannot interview the instructor, you need to question the value of the course.

Create a Relationship with the Instructor Prior to the Course

From a software craftsmanship standpoint, your experienced developers are delegating the training of their apprentices to another person (the instructor), so it is essential that a relationship is established between the instructor and your craftsmen. After all, it is the craftsmen who will have to handle any misconceptions or mistakes that arise when their apprentices take a course. Hence establishing a relationship with the instructor before taking the course is essential; a good instructor makes a big difference in terms of the quality and effectiveness of a course. Talk to the instructor and rate the notes, then allow time for the instructor to fix any issues that might be anticipated. With a good instructor, you won't get substandard notes (a good instructor will typically refuse to use substandard notes), but you do want the notes to be good or excellent.

Follow Up with the Instructor after Each Course

Once the course is completed, make sure that your senior developers talk to the instructor to find out how the course went and ask specifically about difficulties and issues encountered by team members during the course. Similarly, talk to the participants; jointly come up with a way of integrating what was learned into their daily tasks. This follow-up is key because it emphasizes that perpetual learning is important. After all, a short course is irrelevant if the new knowledge and skills are not used on a daily basis so that the way in which participants practice software development actually changes.

If a Course Is a Failure, Fix the Problem

If the course didn't actually work, as you find by talking with participants after the course or noticing developers' inability to apply the new knowledge, you need to take action. If there are only minor problems, your experienced developers might be able to provide sufficient coaching to solve the issues. If the issues are more fundamental, however, run another course with a different instructor. Brief the new instructor about the course that failed, and have her talk with your experienced developers about the unresolved issues and their plans to address them. It might also be useful to talk with the original instructor to find out what went wrong with the first course.

Encourage Your People to Be Visible in the Software Development Community

Once you have all of these learning opportunities in place, encourage your developers to start presenting talks and tutorials, either to the rest of the organization or at local user groups. This next level of learning requires developers to know a subject well enough to be able to present the ideas to other people. At first, it's probably wise to restrict developers to in-house tutorials where the audience is known and the questions should be friendlier. Once a developer has gained confidence as a speaker, then it is appropriate to tackle larger, external audiences.

Encourage Participation at Conferences

Once a developer is comfortable presenting locally, the next step is to start presenting at conferences. For many developers, this step is a daunting one, but it allows good developers to acknowledge their own mastery of the craft of software development. After attending conferences a few times, a developer should identify a topic and write it up as a paper or perhaps propose a tutorial or workshop. Although the proposals might not be accepted initially, even the process of writing up the proposal is useful as a learning exercise.

When a conference accepts a proposal, a developer has a real opportunity to influence the way in which other people develop software. By presenting at conferences ideas about what works for small teams, a developer is redressing the historical balance in favor of software engineering. By opening the conversation from the software craftsmanship perspective, a developer can change the way that software development actually plays out. The price is a fair amount of work in preparing and presenting the ideas, but the payoff is that the ideas become exposed to a wider audience and the resulting feedback serves to improve the ideas.

Encourage Your Developers to Become Instructors

Experienced developers should be involved in the creation of training courses for other developers. As well as getting courses that will be used by a team, they should seek to influence training companies in designing the courses offered. Where possible, they should also get involved as instructors and write courses. We all win from this effort because the courses are created by developers who understand the real issues in software development and are presented by instructors who are working on live projects. Although this is happening to some degree today, from a software craftsmanship perspective too many instructors still have insufficient recent project experience really to understand modern software development practices. Good instructors exist, but all too many have not been recently involved in working as part of a team that delivers useful applications to real customers and users.

Encourage Your Developers to Get Their Ideas Published

A final suggestion for developers is to become involved in the publishing of ideas about software development, either as a reviewer or as an author. Being a reviewer requires less effort; it allows a developer to influence the ideas about software development that appear in print. By providing feedback to authors and publishers, a developer can make suggestions that ensure that the ideas presented are at least compatible with his daily experience. Becoming an author is a much larger step, and getting articles into magazines or writing a book requires a lot more effort. The benefit, however, is that writing requires developers to become very reflective about the software development practices that they use. By taking the time to think through what works and what does not work, a developer can learn a lot. Doing so on a small scale for an article or on a much larger scale for a book turns reflective thinking into a daily habit and in the process moves the developer farther along in the journey of perpetual learning.

Becoming a Reflective Practitioner

Perpetual learning is about challenging all developers to continue to improve their skills. A key problem with the software engineering mindset is that programmers can be misled into thinking that they know everything there is to know about a subject. Software development does not work like that. The field is rapidly changing and evolving. As the power of computing hardware continues to increase even as its price decreases, many of the lessons learned from the early days of computing no longer hold true.[100] Increasingly, good developers are those who can recognize the discontinuities that arise and then create applications that exploit those discontinuities. That effort requires master craftsmen who are perpetually learning and continually pushing the boundaries of the craft of software development.

---

100. For example, we no longer have to write in low-level languages to get adequate performance from our applications. High-level, expressive programming languages now allow developers to be much more productive.

Epilogue

I suspect that the very idea of software craftsmanship may be challenged as a retrograde step by the software engineering community. Craftsmanship diverges from engineering in that it emphasizes personal responsibility and decentralization. Rather than supporting large training and accreditation organizations, software craftsmanship uses apprenticeship to make developers responsible for their own learning. When you hear objections to this discipline, you should ponder first what motivates the objection.

My motivation for writing this book was to question the divergence between what is happening in the application development community and what is recommended in the software development literature. The software engineering-dominated literature just didn't seem to match with the way that good developers were actually shipping great applications.

Eventually I came to see that the real difference was that software engineering was targeted at massive, 100-plus developer-year projects, whereas most application development projects were tiny by comparison. *Software Craftsmanship* is my way of opening up the conversation about what is possible if we choose to develop software using small teams of good developers.

By holding apprenticeship as the way forward for nurturing great developers, I am questioning the value of the schooling approach, which emphasizes short "sheep dip" training courses that dominate the software development world. Has sitting in a lecture hall watching the slides dance by ever been a really effective way to learn?

The decentralized software craftsmanship model is challenging to the centralization of authority, but it is necessary to meet the challenge of the vast breadth and diversity of application development. Rather than trying to improve efficiency through monoculture, craftsmanship seeks to create adaptability through diversity and personal responsibility. In the end, software development is a craft skill that subtly blends art, science, and engineering. It's not just a day job; it can be a passion. I will close this book with my take on process improvement:

Software development is meant to be fun. If it isn't, the process is wrong.

Acknowledgments

Strange as it may seem, this book was actually inspired by the Software Engineering Institute. In the early 1990s, I was searching for ways to improve the productivity of small teams and the Capability Maturity Model looked like a possible starting point. In the end, however, I realized that for most projects, talent matters more than the process that is used.

Very quickly I learned that it wasn't really talent. Great developers were great because they had learned how to create great applications and they were continually learning new ways of delivering great software. I realized then that I owed a tremendous debt to the many software developers and authors whose books populate my bookshelves. Gerald Weinberg, Luke Hohmann, Capers Jones, and Jim Coplien all stand out in my memory for the way that reading their work caused me to stop and think about how to develop great software.

This book has been many years in the making. Alistair Cockburn first gave me the idea that software developers can and should write books. Alistair also encouraged me to become a reviewer for Addison-Wesley, which eventually and indirectly led to this book.

Another indirect influence was Rebecca Bence of Catapulse Inc., who encouraged me to write the article, Software Engineering vs. Software Craftsmanship for the Catapulse Web site. Many of the ideas expressed in Chapter 3 were originally explored in the article, which contrasted the engineering and craftsmanship metaphors.

Many thanks to the team at Addison-Wesley—Mike Hendrickson, Heather Olszyk, Ross Venables, and Marcy Barnes. My reviewers, who gave me lots of great advice, included Ken Auer, Jim Bird, Bruce Brennan, Martin Fowler, Alastair Handley, Andy Hunt, Kim Kelln, Greg Klafki, Michael Le Feuvre, Miroslav Novak, Dave Thomas, Bruce Wampler, and Frank Westphal.

Finally, I want to thank my wife, Lesley, who made me see that it was time to stop complaining about the state of software development and actually get down to writing about the issues. Thanks for your love and support.

Pete McBreen

Index

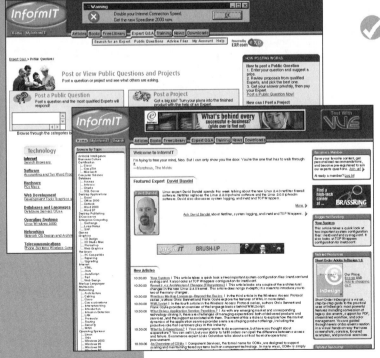

Register Your Book

at www.aw.com/cseng/register

You may be eligible to receive:

- Advance notice of forthcoming editions of the book
- Related book recommendations
- Chapter excerpts and supplements of forthcoming titles
- Information about special contests and promotions throughout the year
- Notices and reminders about author appearances, tradeshows, and online chats with special guests

Contact us

If you are interested in writing a book or reviewing manuscripts prior to publication, please write to us at:

Editorial Department
Addison-Wesley Professional
75 Arlington Street, Suite 300
Boston, MA 02116 USA
Email: AWPro@aw.com

Addison-Wesley

Visit us on the Web: http://www.aw.com/cseng